NEW DIRECTIONS FOR EVALUATION
A PUBLICATION OF THE AMERICAN EVALUATION ASSOCIATION

Gary T. Henry, *Georgia State University*
COEDITOR-IN-CHIEF

Jennifer C. Greene, *Cornell University*
COEDITOR-IN-CHIEF

Evaluation as a Democratic Process: Promoting Inclusion, Dialogue, and Deliberation

Katherine E. Ryan, Lizanne DeStefano
University of Illinois at Urbana-Champaign

EDITORS

Number 85, Spring 2000

JOSSEY-BASS PUBLISHERS
San Francisco

EVALUATION AS A DEMOCRATIC PROCESS: PROMOTING INCLUSION,
DIALOGUE, AND DELIBERATION
Katherine E. Ryan, Lizanne DeStefano (eds.)
New Directions for Evaluation, no. 85
Jennifer C. Greene, Gary T. Henry, Coeditors-in-Chief
Copyright ©2000 Jossey-Bass Inc., Publishers, 350 Sansome Street, San
Francisco, CA 94104.

Microfilm copies of issues and articles are available in 16mm and 35mm,
as well as microfiche in 105mm, through University Microfilms Inc., 300
North Zeeb Road, Ann Arbor, Michigan 48106-1346.

New Directions for Evaluation is indexed in Contents Pages in Education,
Higher Education Abstracts, and Sociological Abstracts.

ISSN 0197-6736   ISBN 0-7879-5371-7

NEW DIRECTIONS FOR EVALUATION is part of The Jossey Bass Education
Series and is published quarterly by Jossey Bass Inc., Publishers, 350 Sansome Street, San Francisco, California 94104-1342.

SUBSCRIPTIONS cost $65.00 for individuals and $118.00 for institutions,
agencies, and libraries. Prices subject to change.

EDITORIAL CORRESPONDENCE should be addressed to the Editors-in-Chief,
Jennifer C. Greene, Department of Educational Psychology, University of
Illinois, 260E Education Building, 1310 South Sixth Street, Champaign,
IL 61820, or Gary T. Henry, School of Policy Studies, Georgia State Uni-
versity, P.O. Box 4039, Atlanta, GA 30302-4039.

www.josseybass.com

Printed in the United States of America on acid-free recycled paper con-
taining 100 percent recovered waste paper, of which at least 20 percent is
postconsumer waste.

Editorial Policy and Procedures

New Directions for Evaluation, a quarterly sourcebook, is an official publication of the American Evaluation Association. The journal publishes empirical, methodological, and theoretical works on all aspects of evaluation. A reflective approach to evaluation is an essential strand to be woven through every volume. The editors encourage volumes that have one of three foci: (1) craft volumes that present approaches, methods, or techniques that can be applied in evaluation practice, such as the use of templates, case studies, or survey research; (2) professional issue volumes that present issues of import for the field of evaluation, such as utilization of evaluation or locus of evaluation capacity; (3) societal issue volumes that draw out the implications of intellectual, social, or cultural developments for the field of evaluation, such as the women's movement, communitarianism, or multiculturalism. A wide range of substantive domains is appropriate for *New Directions for Evaluation;* however, the domains must be of interest to a large audience within the field of evaluation. We encourage a diversity of perspectives and experiences within each volume, as well as creative bridges between evaluation and other sectors of our collective lives.

The editors do not consider or publish unsolicited single manuscripts. Each issue of the journal is devoted to a single topic, with contributions solicited, organized, reviewed, and edited by a guest editor. Issues may take any of several forms, such as a series of related chapters, a debate, or a long article followed by brief critical commentaries. In all cases, the proposals must follow a specific format, which can be obtained from the editor-in-chief. These proposals are sent to members of the editorial board and to relevant substantive experts for peer review. The process may result in acceptance, a recommendation to revise and resubmit, or rejection. However, the editors are committed to working constructively with potential guest editors to help them develop acceptable proposals.

Jennifer C. Greene, Coeditor-in-Chief
Department of Educational Psychology
University of Illinois
260E Education Building
1310 South Sixth Street
Champaign, IL 61820
e-mail: jcgreene@uiuc.edu

Gary T. Henry, Coeditor-in-Chief
School of Policy Studies
Georgia State University
P.O. Box 4039
Atlanta, GA 30302-4039
email: gthenry@gsu.edu

CONTENTS

democratic evaluation are applied in an antidemocratic climate. The case serves to illustrate a theoretical justification and to illuminate strategies for stakeholder inclusion from a deliberative, democratic point of view.

The complexities and confusion surrounding the concept of dialogue in evaluation are analyzed through a critical examination of current theory and practices. A descriptive typology based on genre, process, goal, evaluator identity, orientation, and epistemology is used to analyze two dialogical vignettes. Framing dialogue in this fashion illustrates that it can and perhaps should take more than one form when addressing even a single issue.

Deliberative democratic evaluation and other evaluation approaches that require the linkage of evaluation to social and institutional structures require the application of democratic principles in evaluation and in resulting policy decisions that reflect those ideas. Because democracy in America has been experientially different for certain groups, the challenge is to ensure that members of those groups are a part of the evaluation community.

A critique of the chapters in this volume concludes that the challenges to the pragmatic use of deliberative democratic evaluation are great. Current practice and theory do not go far enough to unmask the potential that evaluation offers for supporting democratic practices and creating democratic communities.

Five themes illustrate different dimensions of the process of diffusing democratic deliberation into more widespread use: appreciation, addition, apprehension, application, and adaptation. The themes raise issues and give guidance concerning evaluation practice and the role of evaluation in society.

Stake challenges a basic assumption of House and Howe, that "evaluation in democratic societies should aim for . . . fostering deliberative democracy." A modest effort by an evaluator to contribute to deliberative democracy is defensible, but vigorous political advocacy violates social expectation.

Editors' Notes

The ten chapters in this volume address issues in democratic deliberative evaluation from both a theoretical and a practice perspective. In Chapter One, Ernest R. House and Kenneth R. Howe present a metaframework based on three features (inclusion, dialogue, and deliberation) that can be used to judge the potential for democratic deliberation in an evaluation. Informed by the House and Howe framework, case studies that consider evaluation as democratic deliberation are presented in Chapters Two through Five. Each case study represents a different context of evaluation as democratic deliberation.

The case studies address several questions from divergent perspectives, including, What is the meaning of and basis for evaluation as democratic deliberation in a particular case? Other questions address the particular strategies, processes, and methods used to advance a specific meaning of democratic deliberative evaluation. The success of strategies, methods, and processes and the barriers to implementing evaluation as democratic deliberation are also investigated.

In Chapter Two, in an evaluation of a local secondary science reform effort, Jennifer C. Greene addresses barriers to implementing democratic dialogue and deliberation. She discusses factors that aided the democratic deliberation of issues, and obstacles that prevented the idealization of democratic deliberation. In Chapter Three, independent practicing evaluator Rosalie T. Torres, along with Sharon Padilla Stone, Deborah Butkus, Barbara B. Hook, Jill Casey, and Sheila A. Arens, examines dialogue and reflection in an evaluation of a family literacy program in which few of the conditions necessary for successful collaboration and participation were present. From the perspective of evaluators working in an internal evaluation unit, Katherine E. Ryan and Trav D. Johnson present in Chapter Four a case study of efforts to open up the conversation about the evaluation of teaching in higher education through dialogue and deliberation. In Chapter Five, Cheryl MacNeil takes up the challenges of creating conditions for deliberative democratic evaluation in an environment that is antithetical to the basic tenants of democracy—the evaluation of a peer-run social service program operating out of a psychiatric institution.

The remainder of the volume is devoted to assessment of democratic deliberative evaluation from several different perspectives. Using the case studies presented in the preceding chapters and other case examples, Katherine Ryan and Lizanne DeStefano attempt in Chapter Six to untangle some of the multiple conceptions of dialogue, a critical feature of democratic deliberative evaluation. In Chapter Seven, Stafford Hood challenges the possibilities of democratic deliberative evaluation in a society in which democracy is experienced differently by specific subgroups (such as people of color). He calls for greater presence of evaluators of color as a means of furthering democratic deliberative practice. In Chapter Eight, Sandra Mathison suggests that the theory and practice of democratic deliberative evaluation proposed in this volume does not go far enough. According to her, the possibilities are great for evaluation to transform and empower lives through the conflation of dialogue and deliberation. While applauding the contributions of House and Howe's approach to evaluation theory, Gary T. Henry, in Chapter Nine, considers several challenges to this approach in practice. These include, for example, how this approach can be adapted in contexts involving geographical distances, and how to separate the collection of information on performance from deliberations concerning values. In the last chapter, however, Robert E. Stake, urges caution in considering democratic deliberative evaluation. From his perspective, the goals of evaluation are more modest than House and Howe's proposal that evaluation ought to foster deliberative democracy.

Katherine E. Ryan
Lizanne DeStefano
Editors

KATHERINE E. RYAN is associate professor of educational psychology at the University of Illinois at Urbana-Champaign.

LIZANNE DESTEFANO is associate professor of educational psychology, associate dean for research, and director of the Bureau of Educational Research at the College of Education, University of Illinois at Urbana-Champaign.

1

Judging evaluations on the basis of their potential for democratic deliberation includes consideration of three interrelated criteria: inclusion, dialogue, and deliberation.

Deliberative Democratic Evaluation

Ernest R. House, Kenneth R. Howe

This chapter presents a framework for judging evaluations on the basis of their potential for democratic deliberation (House and Howe, 1998, 1999). Many evaluators already implement the principles we explicate here without any urging from us. They have developed their own approaches, their own intuitions, and their own robust sense of social justice. Nonetheless, such principles are too important to leave to chance or intuition all the time.

Some people might ask why we need to have an explicit framework that links evaluation to the larger sociopolitical and moral structure. Why can't we just have a pure logic of evaluation or a pure methodology that is removed from the social structure altogether? The answer is the same as to why we cannot have a pure legal system or a pure medical practice removed entirely from the society in which it is embedded.

Evaluation always exists within some authority structure, some particular social system. It does not stand alone as simply a logic or a methodology, free of time and space, and it is certainly not free of values or interests. Rather, evaluation practices are firmly embedded in and inextricably tied to particular social and institutional structures and practices. Otherwise, why would people agree to participate in studies? Why would they fill out surveys or read reports if they were not already part of social practices that condoned these activities? Evaluation resides within an entire social fabric, which influences what is done within the study itself.

Evaluators cannot help but anticipate certain general conditions, mostly as background to the study. They assume particular focuses for their evaluations as background information, to which they often do not give much thought, just as they anticipate when they step out a door that there will be a floor there to prevent them from falling to the next level of the building. It is difficult, perhaps impossible, for evaluators not to anticipate

New Directions for Evaluation, no. 85, Spring 2000 © Jossey-Bass Publishers

general ways in which the evaluation findings will be available, even as they assume that audiences will understand the language of the report. Otherwise, evaluators would collect different data, present it differently, and employ different criteria in some cases. Greene (1997, p. 27) notes that evaluation approaches are "importantly distinguished" by whose criteria and questions are addressed. Different groups require different information, and evaluators should be able to justify why they choose one focus rather than another.

Anticipation of the background conditions of how findings might be used is not the same as evaluators implementing the findings. Scientists anticipate publishing their studies in refereed journals subject to peer criticism without necessarily attempting to put their ideas into practice. They do not anticipate having to pay for publication, for example. Nonetheless, they make assumptions about the ways in which the findings are likely to be received and used. We believe that these background conditions for evaluation should be explicitly democratic so that evaluation is tied to the larger society by democratic principles argued, debated, and accepted by the evaluation community. Evaluation is too important to society to be purchased by the highest bidder or appropriated by the most powerful interest. Evaluators should be self-conscious and deliberate about such matters. A framework and some criteria and checklists are useful to remind evaluators caught in the complexities of difficult evaluations what evaluation in democratic societies should aim for—fostering deliberative democracy, in our judgment.

Deliberative Democracy

Deliberative democratic evaluation may be identified with genuine democracy, that is, with what democracy requires when properly analyzed and understood in its full context. In a sense the term *deliberative democracy* is redundant, because democracy in the fullest sense requires deliberation, in our view. But the redundancy is worth preserving to avoid confusion about our emphasis. We use the modifier to focus attention on the decision-making procedures that democracy requires and to avoid confusion with other conceptions of democracy, such as preferential democracy.

If we look beyond the conduct of individual studies by individual evaluators, we can see the outlines of evaluation as an influential societal institution, one that can be vital to the realization of democratic societies. Amid the claims and counterclaims of the mass media, amid public relations and advertising, amid the legions of those in our society who represent particular interests for pay, evaluation can be an institution that stands apart, reliable in the accuracy and integrity of its claims. But it needs a set of explicit democratic principles to guide its practices and test its intuitions.

The deliberative democratic view is not an evaluation model that prescribes how to conduct an evaluation so much as it is a middle-range theory that suggests that studies should be unbiased (objective and impartial regarding fact and value claims). Bias can never be fully eliminated, but there are specific ways of reducing it. Any number of approaches or models of evaluation or individual studies could fit our middle-range deliberative democratic requirements.

Several evaluators have advocated practices that are consistent in important ways with the views we endorse here, though they might differ in other respects—for example, Stake's responsive evaluation (1984), MacDonald's democratic evaluation (1977), Proppe's dialectical evaluation (1979), Scriven's objective value claims (1980), Greene's advocacy evaluation (1997), and Karlsson's critical dialogue (1996). Fischer (1980); Weiss (1983); Bryk (1983); Mark and Shotland (1987); Garraway (1995); Fetterman, Kaftarian, and Wandersman (1996); Alkin (1997); Schwandt (1997); and Cousins and Whitmore (1998) are other researchers who have explored similar ideas.

In our opinion, there are three requirements for deliberative democratic evaluation: inclusion, dialogue, and deliberation. We discuss each of these requirements in turn, while acknowledging that they are not easy to separate from each other entirely. Then we partially operationalize these principles in ten questions.

The Inclusion Requirement

The first requirement of deliberative democratic evaluation is inclusion of all relevant interests. It would not be right for evaluators to provide evaluations only to the most powerful or to sell them to the highest bidders for their own uses, thus biasing the evaluation toward particular powerful interests. Nor would it be right to let purchasers revise findings so they could delete parts of the evaluation they did not like or enhance the findings with their own self-serving notions. These are conditions of use that evaluators should not condone.

The most basic tenet of democracy is that all those who have legitimate, relevant interests should be included in decisions that affect those interests. This principle separates it from other forms of government. When only a few people decide social policy, an aristocracy, plutocracy, or technocracy exists, depending on whether talent, money, or expertise is the source of authority. We think that evaluation in democratic societies should be explicitly democratic, while recognizing that there are different conceptions of democracy and that evaluative expertise has an important role to play.

Evaluation studies should aspire to be accurate representations of states of affairs, not rhetorical devices for furthering the interests of some groups over others, as in advertising or public relations, with the prize going to those who pay for the service. Genuine democratic deliberation would require that the interests of all stakeholder groups be central and the interests of all relevant parties be represented. If the relevant interests are not considered, we have only a sham deliberation from which some voices have been excluded.

Some of the biggest threats to democratic decisions are power imbalances. Power imbalances are endemic in society, and it is easy to see how they can disrupt and distort evaluations. The powerful may dominate the discussion, or those without power may not be represented adequately. There must be some rough balance and equality of power for proper deliberation to occur. This is true in evaluations as well. Evaluators must design evaluations so that relevant interests are represented and so that there is some balance of power among these interests, which often means representing the interests of those who might be excluded from the discussion, because their interests are most likely to be overlooked. And of course deliberation should be based on discussion of merits, not on the social status of participants.

Determining and weighing interests is extremely complex and uncertain, and often controversial. First, not all interests have the same moral force. Bhaskar (1986) distinguishes interests that attach to needs—the morally weightier type of interests—from the larger array of interests as follows: An interest is anything conducive to the achievement of an agent's wants, needs, or purposes, and a need is anything (contingently or absolutely) necessary to the survival or well-being of an agent, whether the agent currently possesses the needed item or not. Satisfaction of a need, in contrast to fulfillment of a want or purpose, cannot ever, per se, make an individual or group worse off (Bhaskar, 1986). Scriven (1991) advances a similar distinction in the context of evaluation. He distinguishes *value assessment,* in which needs, wants, and market preferences are treated indifferently, from *needs assessment,* properly understood. "Needs," he says, "provide the first priority for response . . . just because they are in some sense necessary, whereas wants are (merely) desired" (p. 241). Needs are associated with a "level of urgency or importance" not possessed by wants, market preferences, and the like, according to Scriven.

We do not mean to suggest that distinguishing interests associated with needs from interests associated with wants is easy to do in the conduct of evaluations, or even always necessary. Still, the distinction is one that evaluators should note. However fuzzy or controversial it is in some cases, the distinction is nonetheless quite real. In many cases it is easy to draw the line, for example, interests in food, shelter, and health care versus interests in early retirement or luxury automobiles.

The Dialogue Requirement

The second requirement of deliberative democratic evaluation is that it be dialogical. What complicates determining and weighing interests is that individuals and groups are not always able to determine their own interests when left to their own devices. They can be fooled or misled by the media, by powerful interest groups suppressing or "spinning" evidence, or by not having or exercising opportunities to obtain information.

The real interests of an individual or group are not necessarily the same as the perceived interests. Real interests might ideally be defined this way: Policy X is in A's interests if A were to experience the results of Policy X and Policy Y and would choose the result of Policy X rather than that of policy Y. Identifying real interests is critical. Choice alone is not necessarily determinative of real interests. It must be choice exercised under the right conditions.

Discovering real interests is a major task of dialogical interaction in evaluation. Evaluators cannot assume automatically what the interests of the parties are. Perhaps the evaluators are mistaken or too distant. It is better to engage participants through dialogues of various kinds. It may be that through dialogue and deliberation stakeholders will change their minds as to what their real interests are. After they examine findings and engage in argument and discussion with others, they may see their interests as different from those with which they began.

The embeddedness of evaluation in the social fabric makes dialogue critical in most cases. Participants and evaluators must identify the real issues and even create them in many cases. Evaluation findings emerge from these processes. They are not necessarily waiting to be discovered, but are forged in the evaluation and discussions of findings.

Of course there is a danger here that the evaluator may be unduly influenced through extensive dialogue with various stakeholder groups, a threat that Scriven (1973) noted long ago in his call for "goal-free" evaluation. Though we believe this threat to impartiality to be significant—that evaluators might lose their impartiality by identifying too closely with stakeholders—the greater danger, in our view, is that evaluators will not fully understand the position, views, and interests of the various stakeholders or groups, or that they will misrepresent them in the evaluation. So we are willing to trade some measure of threat to impartiality for the possibility of better understanding stakeholders' positions by engaging in extensive dialogue with stakeholders. Also, the threat to impartiality should be blunted by including all relevant interests in dialogue.

In some situations there may be little danger of misunderstanding stakeholders' views. Perhaps in some product evaluations evaluators can posit or determine the interests of typical consumers with a minimum of dialogue because the context of the study may be precisely defined in advance. For example, perhaps *Consumer Reports* can capture accurately the views of typical consumers through long practice and interaction with readers.

In most evaluations of complex programs and policies, however, understanding stakeholders and their positions is no easy matter. There may be many stakeholders and issues, and the interests of various groups may conflict. The more complex the situation is, the more dialogue is needed to sort it out. In this sense, product evaluations are more a special case of evaluations than the paradigm case, in our opinion. So we conceive dialogue to be not only desirable but also necessary in most cases.

The Deliberation Requirement

The third requirement of evaluations is that they be deliberative. Deliberation is fundamentally a cognitive process, grounded in reasons, evidence, and principles of valid argument, an important subset of which are the methodological canons of evaluation. In many instances the authority of evaluators, based on their special expertise, plays a critical role in a deliberative democracy.

By contrast, in some other views of democracy, the preferences, values, tastes, and interests of citizens are taken as given and the point is to find ways to maximize those interests. Evaluators cannot question those preferences; they are simply given. In such views, facts lend themselves to specialist determination, as in science, but values are chosen and cannot be dealt with rationally. Hence, the best we can do is satisfy preferences, regardless of what they are. Such reasoning leads to a conception of democracy in which preferences and values are unexamined.

In our view, values should not be taken as given but should be subject to examination through rational processes. Evaluation is a procedure for determining values, which are emergent and transformed through deliberative processes into evaluation findings. Evaluation thus serves a deliberative democracy, one in which interests and values are rationally determined; and careful discussion and determination require the expertise of evaluators, often acting as experts with special knowledge.

To be sure, evaluation should not take the place of voting and other decision-making procedures in a democracy. Rather, evaluation is an institution that produces evaluation findings used in democratic decision-making processes. Evaluation informs voting and other authoritative decision-making procedures in democratic societies; it should not preempt them.

After all, evaluation is inextricably linked to the notion of choice: what choices are to be made, who makes choices, and on what basis. Evaluation of public programs, policies, and personnel is based on the notion of collective choice, and on some sense of drawing conclusions on the basis of merit. By contrast, we can envision individuals weighing and balancing various factors and arriving at conclusions as individuals on the basis of their own interests. This is a model of consumer choice, essentially a market model, with many individuals making their own choices based on available information, and in which collective choice is merely the sum of individual choices.

But most public evaluations are not like this. The relevant interests and stakeholders have to be determined as part of the evaluation, and consumer choice is not the same as collective choice derived from collective deliberation. Collective deliberation requires reciprocity of consciousness among participants and a rough equality of power if participants are to reach a state in which they deliberate effectively about their collective ends.

A note on the evaluator's authority in these matters: It is useful to distinguish between power and authority. Evaluators should accept authority but not power. For example, A has power over B when A can affect B's behavior contrary to B's interests. But A has authority over B when B complies because A has influenced B through good reasons attached to B's own interest. Democratic deliberation exists when deliberations are discussions of merit that involve the interests of A and B or their collective interests. Hence, evaluators have authority in the sense that people are persuaded by the evaluation for good reasons.

The requirements of inclusion, dialogue, and deliberation overlap and crisscross in complex ways. For example, the quality of the deliberation is not separable from the quality of the dialogue, which in turn affects whether inclusion (as opposed to mere tokenism) is achieved. In general, the three requirements of inclusion, dialogue, and deliberation cannot be cleanly distinguished and applied independently. They affect and reinforce one another. Still, distinguishing them from one another provides some guidance as to how an evaluation measures up to the requirements. If the inclusion and dialogue requirements are met but the deliberative requirement is not, all relevant interests might be represented (provisionally) but inadequately considered, thus resulting in erroneous conclusions. If the inclusion and deliberative requirements are met but the dialogical requirement is missing, we might misrepresent interests and positions, resulting in inauthentic evaluations based on false interests and dominated by those with the most power. Finally, if the dialogue and deliberative requirements are met but not all stakeholders are included, the evaluation might be charged with being biased toward particular interests, an inherently undemocratic outcome.

Deliberative democratic evaluation is an ideal worth pursuing, not something that can be achieved once and for all in any one study or fully captured. But then collecting, analyzing, and interpreting data in a bias-free manner so that we arrive at accurate findings is never perfect either. The lack of perfection is no reason to stop trying to do the best we can. There are better and worse ways to conduct studies from the point of view of deliberative democracy.

Implementation

Evaluators conduct their work in concrete social circumstances, and we recognize that the deliberative democratic view is too idealized to be implemented straightforwardly in the world as it exists. An uncompromising commitment to such an ideal would be impractical. However, that the ideal cannot be fully attained does not mean that it cannot be a guide.

Evaluators should not ignore imbalances of power or pretend that dialogue about evaluation is open when it is not. To do so is to endorse the existing social and power arrangements implicitly and to evade professional responsibility. It may be that the existing power arrangements are acceptable, but evaluators should consider this issue explicitly. The solution, in our view, is to face the issues as best we can and to adopt a position of democratic deliberation as an ideal for handling value claims.

In this conception the evaluator is not a passive bystander, an innocent facilitator, or a philosopher king who makes decisions for others, but rather a conscientious professional who adheres to a set of defensible, carefully considered principles for enhancing inclusion, dialogue, and deliberation. We partially operationalize our deliberative democratic view in the following ten questions.

1. *Whose interests are represented?* The interests of all relevant parties should be considered in the evaluation. Normally this means the views and interests of all those who have a significant stake in the program or policy under review.

2. *Are major stakeholders represented?* Of course, not every individual stakeholder can be involved. Usually evaluators must settle for representatives of various stakeholder groups, imperfect though this might be. And no doubt there are also occasions when not all stakeholders can be represented. Representation may mean that the evaluators bring the interests of such stakeholders to the study in the stakeholders' absence.

3. *Are any stakeholders excluded?* Sometimes important groups will be excluded, and most often these will be those without power or voice, that is, the poor, powerless, and minorities. It is a task of evaluators to represent these interests as best they can. After all, who represents the public interest?

4. *Are there serious power imbalances?* In surveying the evaluation it is often the case that particular interests are far too powerful and thus threaten the impartiality of the findings. Often these are the clients or powerful stakeholders who dominate the terms of the study or the views represented in the study.

5. *Are there procedures for controlling the imbalances?* It must fall within the evaluator's purview to control power imbalances. Just as teachers must be responsible for creating the conditions for effective discussion in classes, evaluators must establish the conditions for successful data collection, dialogue, and deliberation. Admittedly this requires considerable refined judgment.

6. *How do people participate in the evaluation?* The mode of participation is often critical. Direct involvement is expensive and time-consuming. It is also potentially biasing. Still, getting the correct information requires serious participation from stakeholder groups.

7. *How authentic is their participation?* Respondents are used to filling out surveys they care little about. As respondents become swamped with accountability procedures, they become more and more careless about their answers. This seems to be a serious and rapidly increasing problem as insincere, cosmetic uses of evaluation result in inauthentic findings.

8. *How involved are they?* Again, although interaction is critical, perhaps there can be too much. Should stakeholders be involved in highly technical data analyses? These could bias the findings. Conversely, superficial or cosmetic involvement and interaction may be just as bad.

9. *Is there reflective deliberation?* Typically evaluators finish their studies behind schedule, rushing to meet an established deadline. The findings are not mulled over as long as they should be, nor is sufficient deliberation built into the study. There is temptation to cut short the involvement of others at this stage of the study to meet the time lines.

10. *How considered and extended is the deliberation?* In general, the more extensive the deliberation is, the better would be the findings we expect to emerge. For the most part, there is not enough deliberation in evaluation rather than too much. The deliberative democratic view is demanding here. But this weighs in with the fact that the most common error in evaluation studies is that the conclusions do not match the data very well.

Let us admit that the procedures and techniques for meeting these deliberative democratic requirements are more raw, untested, and uncertain than the technical data collection and analysis procedures developed over the past many decades. Much work needs to be done, and many evaluators will be less than comfortable blazing new trails in a different dimension. Perhaps gradual testing of new ideas by pioneers is the prudent path. Conversely, no one said that the path to justifiable impartial evaluative claims would be an easy climb.

References

Alkin, M. C. "Stakeholder Concepts in Program Evaluation." In A. Reynolds and H. Walberg (eds.), *Evaluation for Educational Productivity*. Greenwich, Conn.: JAI Press, 1997.

Bhaskar, R. *Scientific Realism and Human Emancipation*. London: Verso, 1986.

Bryk, A. S. (ed.). *Stakeholder-Based Evaluation*. New Directions for Program Evaluation, no. 17. San Francisco: Jossey-Bass, 1983.

Cousins, J. B., and Whitmore, E. "Framing Participatory Evaluation." In E. Whitmore (ed.), *Participatory Evaluation Approaches*. San Francisco: Jossey-Bass, 1998.

Fetterman, D., Kaftarian, S. J., and Wandersman, A. (eds.). *Empowerment Evaluation*. Thousand Oaks, Calif.: Sage, 1996.

Fischer, F. *Politics, Values, and Public Methodology: The Problem of Methodology*. Boulder, Colo.: Westview Press, 1980.

Garraway, G. B. "Participatory Evaluation." *Studies in Educational Evaluation*, 1995, *21*, 85–102.

Greene, J. C. "Evaluation as Advocacy." *Evaluation Practice*, 1997, *18*, 1, 25–35.

House, E. R., and Howe, K. R. "Advocacy in Evaluation." *American Journal of Evaluation*, 1998, *19*, 233–236.

House, E. R., and Howe, K. R. *Values in Evaluation*. Thousand Oaks, Calif.: Sage, 1999.

Karlsson, O. "A Critical Dialogue in Evaluation: How Can Interaction Between Evaluation and Politics Be Tackled?" *Evaluation*, 1996, *2*, 405–416.

MacDonald, B. "A Political Classification of Evaluation Studies." In D. Hamilton (ed.), *Beyond the Numbers Game*. London: Macmillan, 1977.

Mark, M. M., and Shotland, L. R. "Stakeholder-Based Evaluation and Value Judgments." In D. Cordray and M. W. Lipsey (eds.), *Evaluation Studies Review Annual,* no. 11. Thousand Oaks, Calif.: Sage, 1987.

Proppe, O. *Dialectical Evaluation.* Urbana, Ill.: Center for Instructional Research and Curriculum Evaluation, 1979, (mimeo).

Schwandt, T. A. "Evaluation as Practical Hermeneutics." *Evaluation,* 1997, *3,* 69–83.

Scriven, M. "Goal-Free Evaluation." In E. R. House (ed.), *School Evaluation.* Berkeley, Calif.: McCutchan, 1973.

Scriven, M. *The Logic of Evaluation.* Inverness, Calif.: Edgepress, 1980.

Scriven, M. *Evaluation Thesaurus.* Thousand Oaks, Calif.: Sage, 1991.

Stake, R. E. "Program Evaluation, Particularly Responsive Evaluation." In G. F. Madaus, M. Scriven, and D. L. Stufflebeam (eds.), *Evaluation Models.* Boston: Kluwer-Nijhoff, 1984.

Weiss, C. "Toward the Future of Stakeholder Approaches in Evaluation." In A. S. Bryk (ed.), *Stakeholder-Based Evaluation.* New Directions for Program Evaluation, no. 17. San Francisco: Jossey-Bass, 1983.

ERNEST R. HOUSE is professor of education at the University of Colorado.

KENNETH R. HOWE is professor in the School of Education, University of Colorado at Boulder, specializing in educational ethics, policy, and philosophy.

2

Deliberative intentions in an evaluation can be distorted by methodological constraints, stakeholder intents, and evaluator stance.

Challenges in Practicing Deliberative Democratic Evaluation

Jennifer C. Greene

It is widely accepted throughout the evaluation community today that the perspectives and interests of program stakeholders should be included in evaluation work. But which stakeholders? On the basis of what criteria should they be identified and selected? And what does it mean to "include" stakeholder interests and concerns?

The answers to these questions reveal considerable variability in evaluative theory and practice. This variability is rooted in different justifications for stakeholder inclusion (Greene, 1997; Mark and Shotland, 1985). Among these different justifications are the following three, which are presented not as mutually exclusive or even wholly discrete but as distinguishable nonetheless by their major emphases:

1. A *pragmatic* justification for stakeholder inclusion in evaluation has a long and distinguished history. This justification focuses on the practical, often contextual consequences of such inclusion, notably increased utilization of evaluation findings (Cousins and Whitmore, 1998; Patton, 1998), and more recently, enhanced organizational learning and development (Cousins and Earl, 1995; Preskill and Torres, 1998).

2. An *emancipatory* justification for stakeholder inclusion in evaluation focuses on the political location of evaluation in society, on questions about whose interests are served by evaluative discourse and practice. Proponents of this emancipatory stance argue that evaluation is inescapably value based, that the most justifiable values for evaluation are equity and justice, and thus that evaluation can most defensibly serve the interests of those with least power in a given context. Serving such interests most

directly advances the larger goals of equity and justice. So stakeholder inclusion in evaluation with an emancipatory justification is an active vehicle for empowerment and social change (Cousins and Whitmore, 1998; Fetterman, 1994; Mertens, 1999).

3. There is also what I will call a *deliberative* justification for stakeholder inclusion in evaluation (see Chapter One; see also Mathison, 1996; Ryan and others, 1998). This justification links evaluation with the larger sociopolitical and moral structures and institutions of society, and further argues that these linkages should be explicitly democratic (in the sense of genuine, strong, or participatory; Barber, 1984). That is, evaluation should serve to ensure that the program or policy conversation includes all relevant interests and is based on democratic principles of fairness and equity and on democratic discourse that is dialogic and deliberative. Meaningful deliberative evaluation is thus constituted by stakeholder inclusion and emphasizes, to a substantial degree, communicative (versus instrumental) rationality (Benjamin, 1998).

It is difficult to theorize about any of these forms of inclusive evaluation, and even more difficult to practice them. This chapter offers some reflections on one such practice, one evaluation study, that explicitly aspired to be inclusive and to promote democratic dialogue—aspirations that were, however, for the most part, unfulfilled.

The Context: Science Education Reform at Grandview High School

In 1995, in sync with national trends, the Grandview High School Science faculty changed the curricula, instructional strategies, and assessments of their science program. The new science program emphasized science as a process in which students learn knowledge they actively construct rather than knowledge they passively acquire. Program goals highlighted the fostering of scientific literacy and reasoning, in addition to the acquisition of scientific knowledge. The program involved extensive use of hands-on activities and a central role for subject matter with relevance beyond the classroom, such as oil spills and genetic engineering. The new science program also created science classes with more heterogeneous groups of students. Prior to the program change, college-bound Grandview students, with the advice of counselors and parents, chose regents-level science classes or the more accelerated honors-level classes. Students not bound for college took local-level science classes. The new science program merged regents and honors classes into just one level, called honors science. The Grandview science faculty viewed this merger and the resulting student heterogeneity as essential to fulfilling their program goals.

The substantive and pedagogical changes in the science program were nearly universally applauded by the Grandview community. The move to heterogeneous grouping, however, met with considerable controversy. Opponents were concerned that some (honors) children would not be adequately challenged or competitively prepared for college admission, while other (regents) children would experience their science classes as too demanding and difficult. Supporters voiced commitment to upgrading the educational opportunities for poor children and children of color and viewed this detracking move as essential to those ends. On June 4, 1995, shortly after teachers had announced the new program to the community, a national newspaper reported the following:

> For years, Grandview's high school has had a three-tiered system: honors classes for students bound for top colleges, regents classes for those aiming for less selective colleges, and "local" classes for those not likely to go to college. Then, in January, the high school science teachers . . . decided they would merge honors and regents classes starting in September. . . . In the vision they offered, students would be exposed to a richer spectrum of humanity and those with, say, good mechanical intuition could help those more adept at abstract theory and vice versa. . . . The decision . . . produced a powerful outcry [in Grandview, where] the battle has been tinged by class and race. . . . "It's a shameful way to treat bright students," said one parent, a university professor. "They won't be prepared to take science at a top university," said another. [A smaller group of parents and community members] argued that the [existing] hierarchy fostered elitist attitudes [and that] assigning their children to regents classes doomed them to second-class citizenship.

During the early months of program implementation, a November 10, 1995, article in a local newspaper stated the following:

> Opponents of the controversial system of grouping students by ability were bolstered Thursday by a national policy analyst who said it "ghettoizes" education. "It shuts out opportunities for students," said Shirley Malcolm, head of the EHR Directorate of the American Association for the Advancement of Science, who had spoken locally on "Ability Grouping, Science Curriculum, and School Reform," at the invitation of a local college. Her appearance comes amid intense debate in the Grandview school system about grouping science students according to ability. Malcolm made it clear she had not been flown to Grandview as a hired gun by opponents of ability grouping. "I'm not talking about your situation," she said, "I'm talking about the national picture." [Yet] even she acknowledged, "I feel a little like a pig invited to a luau."

Also part of this context is the fact that opponents of detracking in Grandview were vocal, articulate, and skilled in capturing media attention and political voice, while supporters were substantially less powerful and influential. Notably, in the May 1995 Grandview school board election, the detracking component of the science reform was a central issue (as it was again in the board election two years later). In 1995, two of the three incumbents who supported the honors-regents merger were defeated and replaced by two newcomers who opposed the merger. A four-person bloc of opposition became part of the nine-member board.

The Evaluation: An Inclusive and Dialogic Opportunity

In response to this heated public controversy, the Grandview superintendent commissioned a three-year evaluation of the new science program to be steered by a science evaluation committee (SEC) composed of high school science faculty, parents, students, local scientists, and interested community members—a committee that intentionally represented diverse viewpoints and interests. The SEC was charged with assessing the "quality and effectiveness" of the new program while providing "ongoing community involvement and communication." I agreed to be the cochair of the SEC, in large part because the context seemed likely to be well served by an inclusive, dialogic approach to evaluation.

I believed that central to the Grandview controversy about grouping and tracking were differing views and values about which educational outcomes are most important. I believed that some people in the Grandview community valued norm-based individual achievement most dearly, while others valued practical scientific problem solving, and still others valued cooperative student learning or engagement in scientific citizenship. I wanted to use the evaluation to surface and legitimize these differing views and values, to encourage respectful conversations among those holding differing views, and to move them toward shared understandings of valued educational outcomes. That is, I aspired to a form of democratic deliberative evaluation, as advanced by House and Howe in Chapter One. I aspired to an evaluation that begins with the fair and equitable inclusion of all legitimate stakeholder interests and thereby broadens the conversation beyond those who usually speak. In my evaluation vision, these diverse stakeholders are then enabled to voice their varied interests and be heard, to learn about and come to respect the interests of others, and to converse (deliberate) toward some common understandings.

I also believed that the structure of this science reform evaluation context could allow for meaningful implementation of this vision of inclusive, dialogic evaluation. I perceived the SEC as a powerful vehicle for inclusion, because it was created precisely to represent all stakeholder interests. And I perceived the SEC's mandate to provide "ongoing community involvement and communication" as providing significant opportunities for dialogue.

However, the evaluation of the Grandview High School science reform was neither inclusive nor dialogic, neither deliberative nor democratic, despite my repeated and concerted attempts to make it so. An analysis of what blocked these attempts yields, on one level, a simple account of the power of the controlling elites in society. This is not a new or very interesting story, but it is a story with continuing currency and persistent relevance to evaluators who want to promote inclusion, broaden the conversation, and position evaluation as a democratizing discourse practice. Additionally, on another level, this story reveals three critical and interrelated challenges to the democratic ambitions of the evaluation. Understanding these challenges can contribute to improved future practice. In brief, these challenges were as follows:

1. *The absence of significant stakeholder voices.* In this evaluation, significant stakeholder voices were not successfully included. These were mainly the voices of parent and community program supporters, whether their support was for the curriculum change, the detracking change, or both. Some of these voices were those usually left out. I endeavored to create space for these voices not by representing them but by repeatedly underscoring the importance of including multiple concerns, perspectives, and value claims in the SEC's work. But voices that are not present cannot speak, even if an open microphone is available. And voices that do not speak are not heard.

2. *The masking of values by method.* This evaluation used a mixed-method design primarily as a vehicle for incorporating and representing multiple perspectives and values (Cook, 1985). In implementation, however, the deliberative evaluation agenda of directing attention and conversation to these multiple perspectives and values was not effectively advanced. Instead, values and stances became masked by and confounded with method, and familiar debates about methods displaced intended debates about stances and values.

3. *The limited authority of the evaluation.* The authority of the evaluation was bounded and constrained by a host of contextual factors, and its potential influence was thereby undermined. Inclusive, deliberative evaluation requires evaluative authority, even as it risks it by reframing evaluator roles.

Following a brief overview of the evaluation, each of these challenges is elaborated in the remainder of this chapter. Snapshots of the activities of the SEC and excerpts from the public conversations held about Grandview's new science program punctuate the story.

A Brief Description

Despite the considerable stakes involved, the evaluation of Grandview High School's new science program was initiated without funding. All members of the SEC were volunteers and no budget was allocated to the committee. So, after developing an evaluation plan, the SEC next developed a budget and began requesting needed resources from the school district. The budget request was for approximately $20,000 per year; during the first year, the district provided $1,000, which the SEC received late in the school year.

Meanwhile, various SEC members volunteered to conduct various components of the evaluation plan for the first year. Two members, a district administrator and a community scientist, agreed to design and implement the expert scientists' review of the new curriculum. I volunteered myself and the students in my graduate evaluation class to conduct the year-one evaluation of program implementation, involving data gathering from students, teachers, and parents. A parent member of the SEC volunteered to conduct the analysis of standardized achievement test data and grades for year one. A doctoral student in educational measurement also contributed to the year-one evaluation; her doctoral research analyzed student attitudes and student achievement on the performance measurements newly developed by the Grandview science teachers.

So, during the first year of the program (1995–96), the evaluation was conducted largely by volunteer members of the SEC, amid ongoing SEC and public discussions. During the second year of the program evaluation, the SEC analyzed and discussed the year-one data, reanalyzed some data, and painstakingly developed various reports for the community. Although some year-two data collection was planned, it was not implemented because the volunteer capacity of the SEC was fully occupied with year-one analysis and reporting, and because both the district superintendent and the high school principal had left Grandview and interim administrators were even less responsive to continuing budget requests. For the third year of the program evaluation, the new Grandview superintendent became an active participant in the SEC and believed the evaluation to be important enough to allocate funds for selected year-three data gathering and analysis—primarily student and teacher surveys regarding program implementation quality and student achievement test data. An external firm was hired to conduct the year-three data gathering and analysis, under the supervision of the SEC and the superintendent. Reports from year three of the evaluation were available for the school board and the public in May and June of the third year (1998).

Challenges to Democratic Deliberative Evaluation

There are three critical challenges to the deliberative intent of the evaluation. Let us examine each in turn.

The Absence of Significant Stakeholder Voices. *Who is on the committee?* From the outset, the SEC had difficulty filling its designated slots for parents and community members who were supporters of the program and for parents whose children would have been in regents-only science classes. This latter stakeholder group included a disproportionate number of minorities—notably, African Americans, Latinos and Latinas, and poor rural whites. Between ten and fifteen individuals were recruited for committee membership from these identified constituencies, and five individuals actually served on the committee for at least part of a year. But by the middle of the second year, no one from these constituencies was still on the committee, and recruitment efforts stopped (mainly due to fatigue and competing demands on time). No program supporter from the community was ever successfully recruited for long-term membership on the SEC. In contrast, well represented on the committee were science faculty, and parents and community members opposed to the new program, most of whose children would have been in honors-only classes.

Attending to diversity in developing the evaluation plan. At the outset of its work, the committee engaged in an open, iterative process of developing the priority evaluation questions to be addressed and then a plan to address them. As the major facilitator of this process, I steered it toward multiple questions, multiple methods, and multiple criteria for judging program quality. For example, I worked especially hard to ensure that our questions addressed implementation concerns and not just outcomes, that our outcome constructs included attitudes and not just achievement, and that our achievement measures included performance assessments in addition to standardized tests. I was following what I generally believe about good evaluation practice, and I was endeavoring to create space for the unrepresented, unstated, and thus unknown interests of those not present, namely, members of minority groups, parents of regents students, and program supporters. I chose not to try to represent the interests of those not present because I could not claim to know them and did not want to presume to "represent an other" (Fine, 1994). Yet the space created by the calls for pluralism was large, diffuse, hard to define, and even harder to fill.

Here is an example of the kinds of statements I repeatedly made in the Grandview science evaluation, from a letter I wrote to the SEC on March 1996, after the second public forum:

> The multiplism of this evaluation [is expressly intended to] reflect the value pluralism of our society and the local Grandview community regarding the important public issue of science education. [This] pluralism requires respectful dialogue toward balanced and reenvisioned understandings and practices—respectful dialogue that will serve to address questions like, How can the multiple claims and interests that exist be honored and met with the Grandview science curriculum? And how can we balance the needs and interests of multiple public constituencies?

I don't want to suggest that I should not have endeavored to promote a diversity of viewpoints and to create space for them to be voiced and heard in the Grandview science evaluation. I think this was a defensible and appropriate course of action in this context. But creating a space for diverse views is no substitute for direct representation of them, and in the absence of such direct representation, a big space may actually muffle, even mute, the voices of those not there. We must therefore be ever more creative and diligent in including these voices directly. Inclusion is thus perhaps the most important requisite if evaluation is to democratize public conversations about public issues.

The Masking of Values by Method. To fulfill its charge of "ongoing community involvement and communication," the SEC planned periodic public forums. In addition, in my view these forums were also an inventive opportunity to promote democratizing conversations about science education in Grandview. The SEC planned three forums for the first year of the evaluation. The first one, held in November 1995, served to inform the community about the evaluation plan and was relatively uneventful. Actually, anticipating emotional debate and controversy, the committee planned carefully for this first forum. The third forum, initially planned for late May 1996, was not held until year three of the evaluation, because of what happened at the second forum.

The second forum was held in mid-March 1996 for the general purposes of updating the community on our evaluation progress and inviting discussion about that progress. Progress at that time consisted of two sets of information from two evaluation activities. We had preliminary results from an external panel of scientists who reviewed the new science curriculum, and we had primarily descriptive results from science classroom observations. The available results, that is, were preliminary, largely descriptive, and qualitative, and addressed program components other than student achievement. These results came from our intentional use of various evaluation methods as vehicles for capturing multiple experiences and perspectives. The committee, lulled by the calmness of the first forum, did not think this time to anticipate the need to forestall public belligerence. The following appeared in the local paper on March 14, 1996 (the day after the forum):

> Grandview High School parents concerned over this year's merger of science regents and honors classes want to know if the new classes measure up to last year's honors classes. At a Wednesday night meeting, members of the Grandview High School's Science Evaluation Committee had trouble convincing them that a major component of the research will tell them what they want to know. . . . Greene described the research as yielding a depth and variety of student and parent experiences that could only be achieved through interviews, direct observations and narrative reports, balanced by reports from the questionnaires. But parents who spoke at the meeting were more interested in quantified results. Julian R said the Committee needs objective numerical and statistical data on the classes. [Julian elaborated on this in a later electronic communication.] "The real and only issue which this panel has yet to address is whether the students are all effectively learning this material. The basic issue is not content, it is implementation and accomplishment. This can only be established with quantitative testing. . . . Reporting such testing is the only thing that matters to the concerned parents in the community, the rest is fluff." Alex S maintained that Greene's research won't tell parents what they want to know—are this year's classes better than last year's?

As suggested by this newspaper report, the dominant voices in the second forum repeatedly demanded achievement test information, sneered at noncomparative data, and openly denigrated qualitative methods. They did so with excessive rudeness and overt rancor—"Mary T wanted to know whether Greene wanted suggestions from the audience or whether she was there simply to tell them what she was going to do."

The dominant voices in the second forum were those of strong opponents of the science reform's detracking. Their opposition centered around concerns that detracking would "water down" science instruction at Grandview, lower student achievement, and thus undercut student competitiveness for selective college entry. Their stance of program opposition was rooted in the valuing of knowledge mastery and of individual, norm-based student achievement as the most important outcomes of education and thus the most important criteria for judging the success of Grandview's new science program. Believers in this stance also valued standardized achievement tests as the most appropriate measures of these outcomes, and assumed that the previous status quo or the prior science program was an appropriate standard of excellence against which to judge the new program. Illustrations of this stance follow:

> Posted on March 1996 to Schoolnet, a listserv established to facilitate communication primarily among concerned program opponents (caps in original): "THE MOST EFFECTIVE THING WE CAN DO IS TO LOOK AT SAT-II RESULTS IN BIOLOGY AND CHEMISTRY. BY COMPARING SAT-II RESULTS FOR YEARS PRIOR TO THE SCIENCE CHANGES WITH RESULTS FOR YEARS AFTER THE CHANGES, WE CAN OBTAIN AN OBJECTIVE MEASURE OF OLD VS NEW."

> From an interim evaluation report, January 1997: "The purpose of this analysis is to use grades and standardized test scores to see if the change in the science program affected the performance of students."

> Memo to SEC from a community member, March 1996, after the second forum: "The evaluation [must compare] student perceptions of this and last year's science courses. If such comparisons are not made, the evaluation would not provide information on what I view to be the central question: 'Did the change in the structure of the science curriculum improve things or not? Did it impact different groups of students differentially?'"

The Grandview science evaluation, in my vision of it, was expressly designed to provide space for articulation of this and various other stances about priority educational outcomes and accompanying values, and to encourage conversation toward common understandings among the promoters of those stances. But the conversation that happened at the second forum was not about different valuings of different educational outcomes; it was mostly about methods.

Why is this so? Where did the deliberative democratic evaluation agenda of dialoguing about value differences go astray? Clearly, multiple, complex factors and forces contributed to the preoccupation with methods and the rancorous tone of the second forum. I wish to address one such factor at this time, one that I believe has important implications for future deliberative evaluation practice. This factor concerns the disjuncture between the intended values-based dialogue of deliberative evaluation and commonplace, familiar expectations of what evaluation is and looks like.

To elaborate, in consonance with my democratizing ambitions, I wanted the second forum conversation to surface, legitimize, and engage diverse views and values regarding science education in Grandview. The evaluation information that was presented at the forum addressed curricular and instructional quality and featured several different standards for judgment, including those of expert scientists, new state standards for science curricula, and the national science education standards that had been the catalyst for the development of Grandview's new science program. The setting therefore had some potential for encouraging dialogue about these various judgments and standards and their underlying values. But judgments, standards, and values were not the explicit agenda for the forum. Rather, the stated agenda focused on presentations and discussions of data, which are familiar or commonplace evaluation activities. Yet the second forum's data themselves—qualitative interpretive accounts of curricular and instructional quality—were not familiar or commonplace. Thus, for the vocal program opponents, challenges to these data and the methods they represented became the focus of discussion at the second forum. While the vocal program opponents could not easily publicly disrespect values and interests different from their own, they could more easily publicly disrespect evaluation methods they perceived as unscientific. I myself became ensnared in the methods debate myself, thus further legitimizing it.

"Whoever gets to define what counts as a scientific problem also gets a powerful role in shaping the picture of the world that results from scientific research" (Harding, 1991, p. 40). In Grandview, I did not explicitly or publicly define the scientific problem as one of diverse values and visions, even though this was the underlying perspective guiding the evaluation. So participants in this evaluation conversation relied on their own ideas of what evaluation is and should look like. So, instead of a second forum conversation about what constitutes a good science curriculum and good science instruction, sparked by the evaluation results presented but expanding and probing diverse perspectives and stances, the second forum featured a conversation about methods—qualitative versus quantitative. Instead of a conversation that surfaced and legitimized diverse standards and comparisons for judging program quality, the second forum's conversation pitted hard, comparative science against soft, descriptive science. Instead of enabling and promoting diversity, this evaluation's intentional mixing of methods actually served to delegitimize diversity and to provide great hiding places for values. Interests did not successfully displace methods in this conversation; rather, methods masked values.

So, evaluation designs with multiple methods carry not just pluralistic and deliberative potential but also risk. Even more, realization of this potential requires actively displacing the familiar—evaluation as the proper methods, properly applied—with the unfamiliar—evaluation as dialoguing about values and underlying interests.

The Limited Authority of This Evaluation. The end of this three-year evaluation, in the spring of 1998, was a busy time. The external evaluation firm was reporting its year-three findings, both in public meetings and in a series of written reports. Due to time pressures, this firm reported either simultaneously to the SEC and the school board or directly to the board (and to the superintendent, the faculty, and sometimes the interested public). The SEC, that is, never in a position of requisite authority, was pretty much cut out of the loop at the end of this contested evaluation.

Moreover, somewhat independently from the presentations of the evaluation findings, in the spring of 1998 the Grandview school board was considering and voting on various proposals regarding the high school science program. This disregard of data in decision making is certainly not unique to the Grandview school board. In this context, it arose both from the maneuverings of individual board members and their supporters and from the lack of authority accorded the evaluation. As noted earlier, one important factor undermining the evaluation's authority was the turnover in the Grandview superintendent and high school principal positions in the middle of the evaluation. During these administrative transitions, the evaluation was left somewhat adrift, without official sanction or support. A second important factor undermining the authority of the evaluation was the overlapping roles I held in this context, including cochair of the SEC, the primary evaluation expert on the SEC, and one of the actual evaluators during year one. I believe that these roles undermined one another, for example, that my endeavors as cochair to promote pluralism were viewed as partisan advocacy for my own evaluation work, which was largely qualitative and therefore already confounded with stance. The main point here is that my multiple roles further eroded the authority and deliberative potential of the evaluation.

To illustrate the tenor of the conversation about the Grandview High School science program in the spring of 1998, I present the following excerpts:

> Board decision making, as reported in the local newspaper: "Early in April 1998, the Grandview school board passed a resolution to 'restore honors biology' as a separate class [to be called extended honors biology]."

> From a guest editorial by a high school science teacher in the local newspaper, mid-April 1998: "As members of the science department at Grandview High School, we find ourselves deeply distressed by the Board of Education's recent resolution to 'restore' honors biology. . . . First we would like to clarify that honors biology is alive and well at Grandview and does not need to be restored, because it has never been dropped. In fact, it was the regents-level

track that was eliminated from our program three years ago, when all college-bound students were merged into honors-level classes."

From a school board meeting in late April, as reported in the local paper: "After a long and contentious meeting and in a series of divided votes, the Grandview school board approved a string of curriculum changes geared toward improving science instruction. . . . By a 5–4 vote, the board . . . superseded action earlier that created two courses of 'extended honors' biology. . . . While the agenda focused on curriculum changes, the debate among board members and parents had to do with the proper mix of ability levels in science classes."

From beginning to end, then, the conversation in this evaluation context was mainly about who is in science class with whom. I believe that the evaluation's limited authority was insufficient to redirect the conversation to why it matters who is in class with whom, or more substantively, to what kind of science learning we want for our children. I further believe that my insistence on pluralism—which expressed my enactment of an inclusive, deliberative evaluator role—actually decreased the evaluation's authority because it was perceived as partisanship. More generally, in nearly all evaluation contexts, inclusive evaluators need to advocate not for a particular program position but for the inclusion of all legitimate perspectives in an open, fair, respectful conversation (Greene, 1997). But because such advocacy reflects an unfamiliar position; an engaged, committed rather than distant, neutral evaluator stance; and an interactive, dialogic rather than removed, judgmental evaluator role, it is easily mistaken for partisanship, with the consequent erosion of evaluative authority and deliberative potential.

Conclusions

What does all this mean? What are democratic deliberative evaluators to do?

The Grandview science reform evaluation offered a particularly difficult context in which to be an evaluator, especially an inclusive, deliberative evaluator. There were many people in this context who had no interest in or intention of deliberating. There were many people in this context whom no amount of data would convince to change their extreme views. This was not a welcoming or hospitable context for the inclusive, deliberative evaluator. (See Benjamin, 1998, and Vander Plaat, 1995, for excellent discussions on the match of evaluation approach to program philosophy.)

Nonetheless, I would argue that the Grandview context well typifies the kinds of contentious public issue scenarios that could significantly benefit from deliberative democratic evaluation (see also Benjamin, 1998). In Grandview I endeavored to use the evaluation as a platform for promoting inclusive, respectful, and reciprocally educational conversations among all interested and concerned stakeholders. I believed it was critical for people with diverse views on both the substantive science reforms and the grouping change to come together, share, and learn from one another in order to move toward a recognition of the legitimacy of others' viewpoints and of the important need to find some common ground.

Among the evaluation processes and methods employed to promote these conversations in Grandview were the following:

- The SEC itself was a forum for inclusive conversations, because it intentionally represented the multiple, diverse interests that existed in the community.
- The SEC attempted to promote similar conversations in the larger community through a series of public forums planned as open reports on the progress of the evaluation and as open invitations for discussion and dialogue about the meaning and implications of the emerging evaluation findings.
- The evaluation used a mix of methods, because different methods best capture different dimensions of community concerns and because different methods privilege different claims to know.
- All sampling strategies in the evaluation were concertedly directed toward diversity and equitable representation of voice.
- The criteria to be used to judge program quality were intentionally multiplistic and broad, involving, for example, both process and outcome and both standardized and contextualized constructs and measures.

As recounted in this chapter, these strategies met with limited success. The major challenges arose from the failure to include all stakeholder interests, the masking of values by method, and the limited authority of the evaluation. By understanding these three challenges, the experience in Grandview does provide some lessons for the practitioner, notably on how deliberative intentions can easily get distorted. My own future deliberative democratic evaluation practice will specifically endeavor to insist on inclusion and on codes of courtesy in all evaluation conversations, and will seek effective ways to set the agenda explicitly, not to implement the best experimental design possible but rather to "dialogue across differences" (Burbules and Rice, 1991). Stay tuned.

References

Barber, B. *Strong Democracy: Participatory Politics for a New Age.* Berkeley: University of California Press, 1984.

Benjamin, L. "A-Exam." Unpublished manuscript, Department of Policy Analysis and Management, Cornell University, 1998.

Burbules, N. C., and Rice, S. "Dialogue Across Differences: Continuing the Conversation." *Harvard Educational Review,* 1991, *61,* 393–416.

Cook, T. D. "Postpositivist Critical Multiplism." In R. L. Shotland and M. M. Mark (eds.), *Social Science and Social Policy.* Thousand Oaks, Calif.: Sage, 1985.

Cousins, J. B., and Earl, L. *Participatory Evaluation in Education: Studies in Evaluation Use and Organizational Learning*. Bristol, Pa.: Falmer Press, 1995.

Cousins, J. B., and Whitmore, E. "Framing Participatory Evaluation." In E. Whitmore (ed.), *Understanding and Practicing Participatory Evaluation*. New Directions for Evaluation, no. 80. San Francisco: Jossey-Bass, 1998.

Fetterman, D. M. "Empowerment Evaluation." *Evaluation Practice,* 1994, *15,* 1–16.

Fine, M. "Working the Hyphens: Reinventing Self and Other in Qualitative Research." In N. Denzin and Y. Lincoln (eds.), *Handbook of Qualitative Research*. Thousand Oaks, Calif.: Sage, 1994.

Greene, J. C. "Evaluation as Advocacy." *Evaluation Practice,* 1997, *18,* 25–36.

Harding, S. *Whose Science? Whose Knowledge? Thinking from Women's Lives*. Ithaca, N.Y.: Cornell University Press, 1991.

Mark, M. M., and Shotland, R. L. "Stakeholder-Based Evaluation and Value Judgments." *Evaluation Review,* 1985, *9,* 605–626.

Mathison, S. "Evaluation as a Democratizing Force in Schools." *International Journal of Social Education,* 1996, *11,* 40–48.

Mertens, D. "Presidential Address. Inclusive Evaluation: Implications of Transformative Theory for Evaluation." *American Journal of Evaluation,* 1999, *20,* 1–14.

Patton, M. Q. (1998). *Utilization-Focused Evaluation*. Thousand Oaks, Calif.: Sage, 1998.

Preskill, H., and Torres, R. T. (1998). *Evaluative Inquiry for Learning in Organizations*. Thousand Oaks, Calif.: Sage, 1998.

Ryan, K. E, Greene, J., Lincoln, Y., Mathison, S., and Mertens, D. "Advantages and Challenges of Using Inclusive Evaluation Approaches in Evaluation Practice." *American Journal of Evaluation,* 1998, *19,* 101–122.

Vander Plaat, M. "Beyond Technique." *Evaluation,* 1995, *1,* 81–96.

JENNIFER C. GREENE *is professor of educational psychology at the University of Illinois.*

3

Dialogue and reflection among key stakeholders provide efficiencies in evaluation, contribute to its use, and inspire a conviction to take action.

Dialogue and Reflection in a Collaborative Evaluation: Stakeholder and Evaluator Voices

Rosalie T. Torres, Sharon Padilla Stone, Deborah L. Butkus, Barbara B. Hook, Jill Casey, Sheila A. Arens

This chapter examines dialogue and reflection among evaluators and stakeholders in the collaborative evaluation of a family literacy program over a four-year period. The evaluation described here was not undertaken with the particular requirements for deliberative democracy (inclusion, dialogue, and deliberation) recommended by House and Howe in Chapter One of this volume, but it represents one evaluation among those they recognize as using these principles "without any urging from [them]" (p. 3). In our work, House and Howe's criteria for deliberative democracy are most readily seen in the processes of dialogue and reflection among evaluators and stakeholders that were expressly undertaken as part of this collaborative evaluation. Collaborative, participatory evaluation seeks to include program personnel in the evaluation process. That is, program personnel help formulate the evaluation plan, in some cases collect and analyze data, and most often help interpret results and develop conclusions and recommendations (see Cousins, 1996; Cousins and Earl, 1992; Greene, 1988). The evaluation work described here also falls within the current genre of empowerment evaluation (Fetterman, 1994a, 1994b, 1996) and evaluation to support organizational learning (Patton, 1997; Preskill and Torres, 1999; Torres, Preskill, and Piontek, 1996).

The chapter's first section briefly reviews the development of these approaches, what we know about requisites for success, and the benefits of reflection and dialogue. Next, the chapter describes our evaluation work in which dialogue and reflection among evaluators and program personnel were prominent, but in which some of the requisite elements for collaborative, participatory evaluation were not present. These mitigating circumstances reflect House and Howe's recognition that "the deliberative democratic view is too idealized to be implemented straightforwardly in the world as it exists" (Chapter One, p. 9). Our analysis of the circumstances, impact, and shortfalls of the evaluation—based on continued dialogue and reflection among the evaluators and stakeholders involved—both provides deeper understanding of the specific processes undergirding participatory and collaborative evaluation, and is meant to address the lack of stakeholder voices in the literature on evaluation use.

Participatory, Collaborative Evaluation

As the field of evaluation has grown and matured over the last twenty years, the various evaluation approaches mentioned earlier have emerged. In general, their aim is to make evaluation findings more meaningful and empowering to stakeholders, more useful for decision makers, and more effective within an organization. To a large degree, these collaborative, participatory approaches were born out of the need to address the circumstances of traditional early evaluation—conducted by external evaluators who provided summative findings for accountability purposes. In an effort to objectify evaluation, it was distanced from program personnel. But in many cases, this practice mitigated the acceptance and use of findings, even when these findings might well serve more formative or developmental needs. Evaluators, frustrated by their interactions with resistant program personnel and little available evidence that their efforts were serving any real purpose, began exploring and articulating means for increasing involvement and ownership of evaluation processes and findings.

More recently, we have begun to articulate the particulars of participatory evaluation in terms of how evaluators and stakeholders engage. These particulars include dialogue that surfaces multiple points of view that need to be addressed and negotiated, helps make individual and hidden agendas visible, contributes to building a sense of community and connection, enables sensitive topics to surface and be addressed, and facilitates individual, team, and organizational learning (Preskill and Torres, 1999). Reflection, similar to House and Howe's notion of deliberation, is often included within a dialogue. It provides for the review or reconsideration of ideas, assumptions, underlying values, understandings, working hypotheses, and tentative decisions.

Yet the circumstances under which many evaluations are conducted are not necessarily the best for active participation and involvement of stakeholders. Cousins and Earl (1992) point out these necessary components for the approach to become viable: The organization values evaluation, provides the time and resources required, and is committed to organizational learning, and evaluation participants are motivated and willing to learn research skills. Cousins (1996) concludes that the single most important factor in participatory evaluation is administrative commitment. Garraway (1995) criticizes participatory evaluation on at least two accounts: it requires increased time and energy from both the evaluator and stakeholders, and in many cases it offers a facade of empowerment whereby the evaluator gets input from stakeholders but fails to utilize this in any manner that will lead to empowerment. Finally, Preskill and Torres (1999) detail the elements of an organization's infrastructure (leadership, culture, communication, and systems and structures) necessary for successful implementation of a collaborative inquiry approach.

With this review as a background, we now turn to describing a case of participatory and collaborative evaluation, and the results of continued dialogue and the reflection about dialogue, reflection, and inclusion among the evaluators and stakeholders involved.

The Program

The authors (external evaluators, program coordinators, and one person in a dual role) collaborated over a four-year period to evaluate, understand, and improve a multisite family literacy program in Colorado Springs. The following paragraphs provide an overview of the family literacy program's origins and development, which are characterized by expansion through multifaceted programming, multiple funding sources, and across-agency collaborations.

What is now the El Paso County Centers for Family Learning began in 1990 at a single junior high school in Colorado Springs School District 11. Since then it has expanded to six sites, including the original junior high school, three elementary schools in two school districts, one community center, and one Head Start agency. Funding for the sites comes from a variety of federal, state, district, and private sources. The greatest proportion comes from Even Start, which provides federal funds (Title I, Part B) for cooperative projects that build on existing community resources. The goal of these projects is to create a new range of services for early childhood, parent, and adult literacy education.

The six centers provide integrated services to families with children from birth through twelve years of age, including adult basic education, GED preparation, English as a second language, early childhood and school-aged programming, and parenting support. These services are designed to assist parents in becoming full partners in the education of their children, to assist children in reaching their full potential as learners, and to provide literacy training for parents. They are made possible through a collaborative effort of at least seventeen different agencies and organizations.

The Evaluation Work

All programs funded through Even Start are required to have local evaluation components. Although the evaluation work described here satisfied this requirement, it also provided an opportunity for program coordinators to interpret evaluation findings, reflect on their antecedents, deepen their understanding of both the program and their own motivations and assumptions, develop indicated program changes, and gain the conviction needed to actually make the changes.

Characteristics of the evaluation work itself have both plagued and supported it over the past four years. First, relatively little funding was available for conducting this multisite evaluation work for programming to achieve adult, children, and family outcomes. The program has continually struggled to allocate funds so as to maximize the number of sites and families served, and also to support local evaluation work for ongoing learning about implementation and outcomes.

Second, from the outset the work was collaborative, for two major reasons: to maximize its relevance and utility, and to establish ownership for and democratize the evaluation work. The collaboration occurred primarily among the three program coordinators (Stone, Butkus, and Hook), the evaluators (Torres and Arens), and Casey, who over the years functioned in both teaching and evaluation roles. This took place in monthly working sessions characterized by dialogue, reflection, sense making, and consensus on design and methodological issues, interpretation of findings, and next steps.

Third, although it was collaborative among the authors of this chapter, this effort was not as deeply inclusive as it might have been. Due to time and financial constraints, site coordinators, teaching staff, and adult program participants did not participate in the overall evaluation design and interpretation of findings. However, as the evaluation progressed, increasingly we were able to include their voice via data collection activities. That is, initially we sought the assistance of teaching staff in constructing and administering evaluation instruments to adult participants. (In particular, this was undertaken as a cost-saving measure given the limited evaluation resources.) Later we invited the participation of site coordinators in individual interviews, and of teaching staff and adult participants in focus group interviews. During the third year, we received additional state funding to conduct a follow-up study, for which we individually interviewed current and past participants. This brought their voice further into our dialogue about the program. Nonetheless, overall, "inclusion in data collection activities" describes the role of site coordinators, teaching staff, and program participants better than "collaboration in design, interpretation, and actions needed."

Fourth, a fortuitous and pleasing blend of rapport, trust, credibility, and goodwill existed among the three program coordinators and the evaluators at the outset and has continued to grow since then. As we discuss later in the chapter, this has significantly enhanced our efforts, yet in some ways it may have detracted from them as well.

Fifth, over the years the evaluation design and methods evolved, based on some trial and error with methods and what we were learning from the evaluation data. One example of the latter occurred on the basis of a working session conducted in the spring of 1998. We met to review the program's strengths and weaknesses based on findings from the 1996–97 evaluation and the follow-up study mentioned earlier. Through this session we identified lack of participant retention as a major factor mitigating adult achievement—the primary intended outcome of the program and the principle benefit cited by respondents in the follow-up study. To better understand issues around participant retention, we decided to conduct focus groups with the teaching staff from each site. When our dialogue and reflection deepened our understanding of the program's benefits and raised questions around the issue of retention, we realized that focus groups with site staff investigating this single issue would yield more needed information than the paper-and-pencil survey we had intended to do.

The Benefits and Inner Workings of Dialogue and Reflection

As we engaged in continued dialogue and reflection, seeking to articulate the benefits and challenges of this evaluation work and extrapolate its inner workings, we came up with what follows. In these paragraphs we integrate stakeholders' observations and conclusions about our work with specific examples.

Time for Reflection and Sense Making. The single greatest and most obvious value of this evaluation work for the primary stakeholders is that it provided an opportunity for reflection and sense making that would not otherwise have occurred.

> It's always a time constraint not to be able to sit down and say, What in the world are we trying to do here, and are we doing it or not doing it? The evaluation has caused us to reflect; otherwise we don't get to do it. The whole reflection piece is so essential. [Hook]

> We're so overcommitted, so busy, and working so hard to make these programs work for these families that we often don't take the time to step back and reflect on what has occurred and what were the results and how we can make that better. . . .Our times together have given us that . . . so we could make good decisions to move forward. [Stone]

> It allowed us to go beyond the daily details because we are so involved in the day-to-day running of programs that we don't get to sit back and have a vision for the program and look beyond the immediate needs. It was a luxury to be able to schedule the time to do that. [Butkus]

Educators, as most professionals in highly demanding jobs, are in the mode of moving forward without time to reflect. And as Hook has observed, "Evaluation has not typically been something to help you move forward." Indeed, a 1998 synthesis of state and local Even Start evaluations (St. Pierre,

Ricciuti, and Creps, 1998) found wide variation in the quality of evaluations and rare systematic use by Even Start projects "to manage and improve their programs" (p. 25). The dialogue and reflection afforded by this evaluation work invited questions: What do the findings mean? What impact is this having on the program? What can we do about it? Where are we coming from in how we see this? Out of these questions came unforeseen issues, possibilities, and "learning from the process" (Hook).

Learning. Learning occurred on three levels.

1. *Programmatic learning occurred because there was the opportunity for dialogue and reflection to occur, and therefore for insights to emerge, but also because those insights were fueled by the interpretation of systematically derived findings about program processes and outcomes, that is, evaluation data.* "The evaluation findings confirmed what our gut feelings were. . . . We didn't have any confirmation of that in something that was hard and fast. . . .[The data] confirmed what we were already feeling, but gave it credibility. . . . It also gave us specific information to inform program changes" (Butkus).

The resolution resulting from confirmation of informal observations frees thinking about the program to move into areas of new learning and action. For instance, our positive assessments about adult learning and benefit were confirmed by statistically significant gains in measures of basic skills and English language skill, and by findings from the follow-up study.

> Internally, we know that if people come and if people stay it impacts families.
> To have that confirmed over a three-year period was good [Stone].

This confirmation led us to focus on the issue of participant retention described earlier. Through our analyses and interpretation of staff focus group data, along with participants' articulations of program benefits, we arrived at an overarching, mediating theme of *connection* with program participants as essential for improving retention and ultimately for program success.

We saw that virtually all aspects of the program could be examined in terms of increasing the connection with participants, and thus the likelihood that they would find it satisfying and give it priority among the competing demands of their typically complicated lives. This comprehensive look at the relationship between participants' connection to each aspect of the program "brought the program to a focus . . . looking at how students can be retained" (Stone). It helped the program coordinators "examine the structure of the program . . . the importance of connection with staff, and how this [connection] could be provided in the program hours" (Butkus).

2. *Development of this overarching theme was the focal point for learning about underlying values among the program coordinators and evaluators.* We developed a comprehensive set of recommendations to foster connection with participants in all program areas. At the same time we recognized that enacting the recommendations would require adequate resources, and

that improvement in program outcomes would require increased attention to program quality rather than increasing the numbers of sites and participants served. Although these conclusions seem logical enough, arriving at them meant grappling with implicit values that many educators hold but do not necessarily examine critically.

> The question, "Are we trying to do too much with too little?" . . . is really an overriding issue for me that has really helped me. I tend to be . . ."Oh, we can do anything, anytime, anywhere, anyhow." And the reality is we can't. . . . Coming face to face with that has been a little bit hard I think. . . . Knowing that we have limited resources and . . . limits as individuals. . . . Had we not been around the table talking in doing this evaluation, then the whole thing of trying to do too much would not have come up [Stone].

> Trying to do too much on too little was kind of a novel thought—for the three personalities that were working on that [Butkus].

> We often leap into "more is better" [rather than quality is better] because we're spreading the word [about family programming]. . . . I think that without the ability to learn what we were doing and what the essential piece was—to help this program be what it needed to be—I don't think we could have pulled back from the "more is better . . . "because we wouldn't have had any foundation for it [Hook].

> These realizations led to conviction about focusing the entire cross-agency collaboration on quality over quantity. When we could see that if retention became one of our primary focuses that meant we were improving what we were doing and because that was crystal clear, we cared more about that particular thing. . . . That was essential for me particularly as I was working with the other partners who wanted to expand. . . . We were able to say, "And if you wish to expand, this is the kind of money you will have to put forth. The money we have can't be stretched any more.". . . I never could have done that otherwise [Hook].

3. *In the course of this work, learning about evaluation that incorporates extensive dialogue and reflection occurred.*

> I had never seen an evaluation [proposal] written like that before. I was pretty struck by what an evaluation could mean. I had never seen anything written that was collaborative. Every evaluation I had ever looked at was tests and outcomes. . . . I thought, "Oh, this could actually be participatory" [Stone].

> My experience and understanding of evaluation in the past has always been very detached from the real programming . . . so going into the thought of an outside evaluator is just one more person taking a piece of what we're doing

and giving us some numbers. But what I found the process to be is one where we're really looking at all of the ins and outs of the program, all of the pieces, and looking at all aspects . . . which is quite different from what I anticipated going in. . . . Another thing that the evaluation process became that I didn't expect was the time to reflect [Butkus].

We've been through so many evaluations and the findings were so ho-hum. The people who were evaluating didn't have any buy-in . . . and what happens for me is it gets shelved. But the other piece of learning this evaluation pointed us to, when we sat together, is much more valuable than ever would have appeared to me at the beginning. Because the questioning and dialogue made us sit back on our heels and assess—that was as valuable as anything, as any part of this evaluation [Hook].

From the evaluator side, we have come to understand more specifically what our role means in facilitating this work. It has included the traditional work of providing technical expertise and assistance in evaluation design, methods, and analysis; but it has also included taking care to create an iterative process in which we review what has gone before, connect what we are learning to what we already know, offer ideas and observations about what findings mean and about indicated programmatic action, construct conceptual frameworks to guide the inquiry process and to make sense of findings, and exercise judgment about what level of analysis and presentation data are appropriate to be maximally useful. Ultimately this is an evaluation role that more so than ever before bridges program and evaluation work, and as such is a role not all evaluators and stakeholders may embrace.

Efficiencies. Although dialogue and reflection within an evaluation may require the dedication of additional time for this purpose, we did realize certain efficiencies from it. First, it served as an additional means of data collection. In the course of deliberating over findings and their antecedents, program staff often provided additional information about implementation that was not otherwise available through formal data collection activities. This was of particular help given the complexity of programming that addressed three major target groups (children, adults, and families) and spanned up to six sites, each varying slightly in the particulars of implementation. Additionally, having one of us serve in both program staff and evaluation roles helped bridge communications and the conveyance of information helpful in carrying out specific evaluation activities (such as drafting instruments, analyzing data, and drafting reports).

A second efficiency was help for program coordinators with planning and articulating next steps:

There is efficiency in planning because certainly, certainly, you don't waste time. If you have taken the time to reflect, if you have taken the time to question, and if you've taken the time to work on where you need to be, where you are now, and how you are going to get there, it is much more efficient to plan. I mean, it kind of all falls into place [Hook].

Relationship. The spirit of inquiry that pervaded our dialogue and reflection was possible first and foremost because of the rapport, trust, and credibility that exists among the evaluators and program staff. There is some prior history. Formerly, the senior author had worked as an internal evaluator for Colorado Springs School District 11 (although none of us had worked together directly before). So we do not have much to say about how to build rapport, trust, and credibility initially—except that it serves this work well and underscores the importance of a "caring connection" that we also learned about as we sought to understand means for enhancing participant retention.

We did take the opportunity of writing this chapter to examine whether (and if so, in what way) our continued work together had deepened the connection. We concluded that it had, particularly among the program coordinators.

> I always had a lot of trust and faith in Barbara and Debbie, but I do think that sitting down and having the time to reflect solidified that for me . . . that these are people I further trust and depend on . . . just being able to sit with everybody and process this kind of [evaluation] information [Stone].

> It helped us to continue to grow the respect we have for the women in the group, and to see them for the visionaries they truly are. I always came from our sessions feeling really, really good. I always knew there was more work to be done, but I felt like we had direction [Butkus].

Thus we have come to understand better how discussion "is an important way for people to affiliate with one another, to develop the sympathies and skills that make participatory democracy possible. . .," and "acts as a catalyst to helping people take informed action in the world" (Brookfield and Preskill, 1999, p. 7).

Concluding Thoughts and Considerations

The benefits we realized from this evaluation work—time for reflection, learning on numerous levels, efficiencies in data collection and program planning, deepened professional and personal relationships, and the conviction to take action—were possible because arguably the single most important requisite for collaborative, participatory evaluation was present from the outset: administrative and leadership commitment to evaluation for the purposes of learning and improvement. This commitment provided the space (that is, motivation and basic resources) in which significant dialogue and reflection, and deliberation could occur.

What we did not have was sufficient resources for wider stakeholder inclusion in the evaluation design or the major work on interpreting findings. As the evaluation progressed over the years, the voices of other stakeholders were represented through findings from focus groups and individual interviews with them. Yet we know that their direct involvement in our dialogue and reflection would have further sensitized us to the exigencies of daily operations of the program and helped us make sense of disparate sets of findings. It would have, as House and Howe advocate, increased the possibility of "fully understanding [their] positions" (p. 7). It would have further democratized the evaluation processes, and appropriately so because decisions made and actions taken had impacts on a wider range of stakeholders.

We recognize too that as a group we constantly faced the challenge of scheduling enough time together given everyone's multifaceted and demanding work. Then, when we got together, the complexity of the program often gave us too much to wrangle with in the time available. Adding others would have slowed down the work more, for two reasons. First, additional participants, rightfully so, would have brought additional perspectives and information to be taken into account and reconciled in the work of the group. Second, additional participants would have changed the dynamic of the group. It would have taken time for a new dynamic to emerge—one that might not have felt ultimately as satisfying and productive as the present one did. We feel it is important to recognize that by not being more inclusive, we cannot fully know what we missed. And maybe, too, some part of us did not want to face that transition time when additional members join a group and the resultant new dynamic is uncertain. When the rapport, trust, and camaraderie are good, it is a fabulous thing; but it is also a good thing to check in on from time to time, and to be willing to risk in the interests of inclusiveness.

As mentioned earlier, this work was not undertaken with explicit acknowledgement of House and Howe's criteria. Yet our experience confirms much of what they would have us believe is true. Evaluation findings emerge from dialogue whereby evaluators and participants construct meaning. The threat of co-optation from evaluators identifying too closely with stakeholders is outweighed by the depth of understanding that extensive dialogue affords. Deliberation requires equality among participants. Although evaluators should not have power over other participants, they can and should exercise the authority of the evaluation—that is, its influence for the betterment of all.

In this review of our work, we surface more than House and Howe tell us about the impact of dialogue and reflection on ongoing learning and subsequent action. We have seen for ourselves how dialogue and reflection—whether about modifying the program or redirecting the evaluation—give participants greater understanding, confidence, and conviction about the objects of discussion, which in turn increases the likelihood that informed change will occur. It empowers participants to enact change on the basis of program issues and evaluation findings that have been thoroughly considered. Further, provided that there is adequate inclusion, the resultant interpretations, understandings, and convictions need not be devoid of the voices of those who are affected by the changes.

We cannot help but feel that our work is part of current change within the evaluation of comprehensive, community-based efforts described by Schorr (1997, p. 138): "The evaluation world is being demystified, its techniques becoming more collaborative, its applicability broadened, and its data no longer closely held as if by a hostile, foreign power."

Part of this demystification is reflected in the evaluator's role in dialogue and reflection. It is yet very much a specialized role, but because that role is to help facilitate questioning, the reduction of information, and authentic sense making for participants, it feeds equity, democracy, and empowerment within the group.

Toward this end we offer these thoughts and questions for evaluators and stakeholders seeking the benefits and challenges of dialogue, reflection, and inclusion within collaborative, participatory evaluation:

- Time for reflection and dialogue needs to be explicitly scheduled as part of the evaluation.
- Dialogue and reflection about evaluation findings, in particular, can readily blur the boundaries between program and evaluation; evaluators and stakeholders need to consider at the outset which are the appropriate boundaries to ease and which are the ones to retain.
- Depth in participation versus breadth in inclusion must be considered by asking, What's the right balance to support stakeholders' participation—and particularly when resources are limited?
- As many evaluators have learned, facilitating dialogue and reflection within a heterogeneous group requires greater skill in facilitation and mediation than traditional evaluation training typically provides.
- Finally, negotiating access to a wide range of stakeholders requires some effort; many evaluation clients and stakeholders may have limited experience with opportunities for expanded interaction within the context of an evaluation and may not readily see why they should devote time to participating.

Despite these unresolved issues, questions, and potential trouble spots, based on our experiences we are more inclined than not to trust the processes of dialogue and reflection. For us, "participating is really believing" (Hook).

References

Brookfield, S. D., and Preskill, S. *Discussion as a Way of Teaching: Tools and Techniques for Democratic Classrooms.* San Francisco: Jossey-Bass, 1999.

Cousins, J. B. "Consequences of Researcher Involvement in Participatory Evaluation." *Studies in Educational Evaluation,* 1996, 22, 3–27.

Cousins, J. B., and Earl, L. M. "The Case for Participatory Evaluation." *Educational Evaluation and Policy Analysis,* 1992, *14,* 397–418.

Fetterman, D. M. "Empowerment Evaluation." *Evaluation Practice,* 1994a, *15,* 1–15.

Fetterman, D. M. "Steps of Empowerment Evaluation: From California to Cape Town." *Evaluation and Program Planning,* 1994b, *17,* 305–313.

Fetterman, D. M. *Empowerment Evaluation: Knowledge and Tools for Self-Assessment and Accountability.* Thousand Oaks, Calif.: Sage, 1996.

Garraway, G. B. "Participatory Evaluation." *Studies in Educational Evaluation,* 1995, *21,* 85–102.

Greene, J. C. "Communication of Results and Utilization in Participatory Program Evaluation. *Evaluation and Program Planning,* 1988, *11,* 341–351.

Patton, M. Q. *Utilization-Focused Evaluation.* (3rd ed.) Thousand Oaks, Calif.: Sage, 1997.

Preskill, H., and Torres, R. T. *Evaluative Inquiry for Learning in Organizations.* Thousand Oaks, Calif.: Sage, 1999.

Schorr, L. B. *Common Purpose: Strengthening Families and Neighborhoods to Rebuild America.* New York: Anchor Books, 1997.

St. Pierre, R. G., Ricciuti, A. E., and Creps, C. *Summary of the State and Local Even Start Evaluations.* Cambridge, Mass.: Abt Associates, 1998.

Torres, R. T., Preskill, H., and Piontek, M. E. (1996). *Evaluation Strategies for Communicating and Reporting: Enhancing Learning in Organizations.* Thousand Oaks, Calif.: Sage, 1996.

ROSALIE T. TORRES *is director of research and evaluation at the Developmental Studies Center in Oakland, California.*

SHARON PADILLA STONE *is director of adult and family education for Colorado Springs School District Eleven.*

DEBORAH L. BUTKUS *is a family literacy specialist for adult and family education in Colorado Springs School District Eleven and director of the Even Start Program.*

BARBARA B. HOOK *is former director of the Office of School Community Relations for Colorado Springs School District Eleven and project comanager of the El Paso County Centers for Family Learning.*

JILL CASEY, *formerly a teacher with the El Paso County Centers for Family Learning, is currently a research assistant at the Developmental Studies Center in Oakland, California.*

SHEILA A. ARENS *is a doctoral student in educational psychology at Indiana University, Bloomington.*

4

The way in which participation is constructed by the evaluator and perceived by the participants was found to influence evaluation impact.

Democratizing Evaluation: Meanings and Methods from Practice

Katherine E. Ryan, Trav D. Johnson

What should evaluation theory and practice look like during the late twentieth century in a democratic society? House and Howe (1998) propose a deliberative democratic evaluation theory and practice that reflects the society in which it is embedded—a society that advances democracy. Acknowledging the reciprocal relationship between evaluation and society, they further suggest that "evaluation . . . can be vital to the realization of a democratic society" (p. 2). This link is made explicit when evaluations are based on principles of deliberative democracy.

How is this to be accomplished? House and Howe (1998) present an overall framework for judging evaluations on the basis of their potential for democratic deliberation. According to them, democratic deliberative evaluation is characterized by three dimensions: deliberation, inclusion, and dialogue. *Deliberation* is defined as reasoning reflectively about relevant issues, including the identification of preferences and values. *Inclusion* is defined as including all relevant interests, stakeholders, and other citizens with specific concerns. The approach is also dialogic. Stakeholders and evaluators engage in *dialogue* during the evaluation process. Through dialogue, stakeholder interests, opinions, and ideas can be portrayed more completely.

The ideology of House and Howe's theory is clear. (See Greene, 1997, and Mathison, 1996, for similar discussions of some form of democratic evaluation.) These theories propose addressing complex issues in evaluation through commitment to some form of democratic principles. These issues include influencing the decision making in the evaluation process and beyond, contributing to more fair and just social practices and institutions, locating stakeholders and constructing valid representations of the stakeholders' viewpoints, and linking the results of the evaluation to action.

While democratically oriented evaluation approaches have significantly advanced evaluation theory, there is a lack of concrete, specific strategies for dealing in practice with the complex issues these approaches address. Further, the advantages and challenges of implementing deliberative democratic evaluation have not been addressed. How does deliberative democratic evaluation fare in practice? Take higher education as one example—how might evaluations in this setting address the ideals of democracy?

While Goodman (1962) and Wolff (1969) have proposed that an authentic community of learning is democratically self-governed by groups of scholars, universities are usually governed by boards and a hierarchical administrative structure. As a consequence, although faculty senates and committees serve in advisory roles, members of the community of learning are not necessarily included in decisions on issues that are critical to their interests (Gutmann, 1987). What would be the benefits of more democratization than now exists in higher education? Gutman suggests that" participation can improve the quality of decisions by universities on many significant issues, it can be educationally valuable for students, it can make both faculty and students more committed to the university's educational purposes and more united in what those purposes are" (p. 191).

Furthermore, what does participation mean to internal evaluators working in a special evaluation unit in higher education? How would participation in evaluation be conceptualized and operationalized in this setting? Could implementing this kind of approach address some of the prominent issues identified with internal evaluation (such as the bureaucratization of evaluation, addressing questions of interest to management while excluding other groups, and the conflict between being critics and advocates) (Mathison, 1991a, 1991b)?

We have written this chapter from the perspective of evaluators working in an internal evaluation unit.[1] We present the results of an *instrumental case study* (a case studied to elaborate or modify theory) (Stake 1994, 1995). We use the *grounded theory approach* as an analysis strategy by comparing and contrasting House and Howe's theory against the data we collected (Strauss and Corbin, 1994). In using the grounded theory approach, we identified a set of issues connected to participation and its representation and the role of the internal evaluator that extends House and Howe's theory. Specifically, we report on our attempt as internal evaluators to shift the evaluation of teaching from a hierarchical evaluation approach to a deliberative democratic evaluation of teaching characterized by inclusion, dialogue, and deliberation. We use these dimensions for judging democratic deliberation proposed by House and Howe as a framework for interpreting the project.

What do we mean by democratizing the evaluation of teaching? In the context of this study, it involves finding stakeholder groups and perspectives (more than are usually included) and ensuring that these stakeholder groups are constructed and represented in conversations and decisions in some fashion. Further, democratizing the evaluation of teaching involves all stakeholders in deliberation about public issues, and seeks direct participation by the members of stakeholders groups in all phases of the evaluation process, including an examination of preferences and values.

The chapter is organized as follows: We provide a brief description of the current teaching evaluation system and discuss some of the issues of the current approach. House and Howe's dimensions of inclusion, dialogue, and deliberation are defined within the context of the study. We report on the implementation of these dimensions in our attempt to democratize evaluation. After discussing several issues we encountered in implementation, we close by returning to House and Howe's theory. We discuss the implications of the findings of our study for the theory and practice of deliberative democratic evaluation.

Background and Context of the Study

In 1994, as internal evaluators in the evaluation division of the Office of Instructional Support and Improvement, which is housed within Academic Affairs under the provost's office in a large midwestern university (hereafter referred to as Midwestern University), we began a study on the evaluation of teaching. As at most colleges and universities, the primary approach to evaluating teaching effectiveness at this university was student ratings of instruction. The current student ratings system, the Teaching Evaluation System (TES), was developed in 1978. The original intent of the TES was to provide formative evaluation to faculty about teaching. Originally, faculty committees were involved in the development of TES. Nevertheless, over the years, as the press for accountability increased within higher education (Gray and Diamond, 1994), the evaluation information from TES began to be used for promotion, tenure, and salary purposes.

TES had become standard operating procedure (Braskamp, Brandenburg, and Ory, 1987; Mathison, 1991b). With SOP, the types of information collected is standardized (e.g., scores on standardized tests, student ratings) and resembles management information systems (Mathison, 1991b). At the same time, the opportunity for other types of information to be collected is decreased. This effectively reduces the conduct of evaluation to what Schwandt (1989) calls *evaluation technology*. Evaluation technology is the development and execution of a set of procedures that serves the "administration of social affairs" (p. 14). TES, to a great extent, fit this description. What started as a primarily horizontal formative evaluation system designed to be responsive to faculty concerns about the evaluation of teaching was transformed over the years into a hierarchical, summative, evaluative, campuswide system for evaluating teaching.

Dimensions of Democratic Deliberative Evaluation

Inclusion. "Is there, then, an ideal university community according to democratic standards? Yes and no. To the extent that there is an ideal community, it is one whose members are dedicated to free scholarly inquiry and who share authority in a complex pattern that draws on the particular interests and competencies of administrators, faculty, students, and trustees" (Gutmann, 1987, p. 193).

Although historically faculty members at Midwestern University were involved in deciding how teaching should be evaluated, in the 1990s there was little institutional capacity for their inclusion in this process. There was no way for faculty to address in a systematic way concerns about the evaluation of their teaching. Furthermore, the faculty could not be considered a single homogeneous stakeholder group. In fact, there were stakeholder groups among faculty who had specific issues of concern. For instance, some faculty expressed concern about whether members of specific subgroups were rated differently than members of other groups. Examples include such diverse groups as men and women, minorities and nonminorities, and groups divided by discipline. The concerns of the engineering faculty are illustrative. The engineering faculty were concerned that they were rated more harshly because their courses were more "difficult" than other disciplines, such as the humanities.

Where were the students in this process? Occasionally the students raised issues about public access to the results of student ratings through the student newspaper or the student government association. We did not initially identify students as a stakeholder group; the salience of their concerns and interests became more apparent as we reflected on how to democratize the evaluation of teaching. Whether students can judge teaching effectiveness is a controversial issue; nevertheless, their stake in teaching is difficult to dispute. As a consequence, we identified them as stakeholders and sought their perspective on the evaluation of teaching. The parents of students as well as interested citizens who were not included are also potential stakeholder groups.

What about other stakeholders and the "client"? For the most part, other stakeholder groups, such as administrators (dean's and department heads), found information from student ratings adequate for addressing personnel issues. Who is the client? The provost's office is representative of the trustees' interests. Historically, the internal evaluator was closely aligned with management. Consequently, from the perspective of the traditional role of the internal evaluator, the provost's office is the client, because the internal evaluation unit is located within Academic Affairs.

Dialogue and Deliberation. "The sheer size of multiversities[2] makes it difficult for faculty and students in multiversities to share in policymaking or even be consulted before others make policy" (Gutmann, 1987, p. 191).

We began a dialogue with faculty by asking several questions about the primary approach to the evaluation of teaching on campus: student ratings. The study focused on two issues: the extent to which faculty found the current TES instructor report useful and easy to interpret, and the extent to which faculty used findings from the TES report to improve their teaching. Data were collected by two methods: questionnaires and focus groups.

Questionnaire. A very short instrument composed of Likert-type and open-ended items was developed. The questionnaire was included with the instructor reports generated for Midwestern University teaching faculty (assistant professors, associate professors, and professors) in late May 1996 (N = approximately 2,100). A follow-up questionnaire was also sent. In all, 268 questionnaires were returned from both mailings (a return rate of 13 percent).[3]

Focus Groups (Faculty). Several prototypes of reporting systems for teaching evaluations were developed. In addition to the current reporting system, two prototypes were reviewed by several focus groups. Members of the focus groups were selected from across some of the diverse faculty groups.[4] For example, the college groups were a proxy of the faculty groups divided by discipline.

Focus Groups (Students). Five student focus groups were conducted to find out about students' perspectives on the evaluation of teaching. The focus groups included classes from different colleges (Applied Life Studies and Liberal Arts and Sciences) and levels (introductory courses, general education, and graduate-level courses).

Faculty Committees. To involve faculty members directly in deliberation, we created committees in which faculty could convene to address evaluation design and broad policy issues surrounding information obtained from existing and new evaluation approaches. These faculty committees were the primary vehicle for involving faculty in decision making. We acted as facilitators of these ongoing discussions to summarize main points and introduce new issues identified by faculty. Two committees were formed:

1. *TES faculty review committee.* To increase faculty involvement in making policy regarding the use of TES for development and personnel decisions, the TES faculty review committee was formed to increase faculty involvement in this area. This committee is composed of faculty across campus who have agreed to participate in revising the current TES and to plan for new directions in course evaluation. Ten faculty members are on the committee.[5]

2. *Evaluation on-line (EOn) development committee.* EOn is an effort to develop a Web-based course-evaluation system for use in on-line courses. Decisions in the development of EOn have been turned over to faculty through an e-mail discussion group (the EOn Development Group) of interested faculty members.[6]

Interpretation: Asking the Wrong Questions the Wrong Way and Getting Some Right Answers

A questionnaire is quite limited for engaging in dialogue. Because there was no opportunity to probe for clarification, we needed to ask more global questions. We asked narrow questions about TES on the questionnaire. Essentially we asked faculty what was wrong with the report on the questionnaire items' scales. In their responses to the open-ended questions, they told us that the report was not the real problem (for example, "You are asking the wrong questions on the questionnaire"). The faculty suggested that they were more concerned with how their teaching effectiveness was being represented. In addition to minimal opportunity for dialogue, there was no opportunity for deliberation, that is, for reasoning, reflection, and debate. Furthermore, the response rate was low; many chose not to participate.

The faculty focus groups did allow for some dialogue and an examination of preferences and values. As a consequence, faculty members' perspectives were clarified (for example, they indicated little interest in having their teaching compared to other faculty; they preferred some type of standard instead). However, to some extent it is more difficult to be inclusive with focus groups. Not all faculty members can participate nor can all groups participate. The influence of differential power relationships is also a potential problem in the focus groups. For instance, during the College of Engineering and College of Communication focus groups, the faculty members spoke freely about their concerns about student ratings. There was a distinct difference in how faculty portrayed their views on the evaluation of teaching when the dean of the college also attended the focus groups. When open-ended questions were posed by the evaluators, there was silence. No faculty members responded. Finally, a few faculty members did respond to specific questions involving different report formats. When the dean was present, the faculty members did not seem as free to express their concerns about how teaching effectiveness is portrayed on the campus.

The student focus groups provided a different venue for students' voices. However, we found that most students were not informed about student ratings. They were concerned about whether and how student rating results were being used. They were pleased to be asked about them.

Opening Conversation about the Evaluation of Teaching

The EOn discussion group seems a most promising way for faculty to be involved in dialogue and deliberation about the evaluation of teaching, including an examination of preferences and values. This discussion initially took place through e-mail and later on WebBoard, an on-line conferencing tool. Because this was a new initiative, faculty had considerable flexibility in making decisions on the development and implementation of the new system. People did not have to be gathered together in one place to discuss something. Having learned from asking the "wrong" questions on the questionnaire, we posed open-ended questions in our roles as facilitators.

In examining the dialogue and deliberation in e-mail comments of the EOn Development Group, we found two distinct perspectives. Initially, the *traditionalist perspective* (in favor of traditional student ratings approaches except on-line) dominated the discussion. Following is an excerpt of this part of the dialogue:

> "My preference is therefore that all on-line forms have the two standard items currently preprinted on all TES forms" (Oct. 12, 1999, male full professor, finance).
> "I agree with [the finance professor]" (Oct. 12, 1999, male lecturer, MBA program).
> "A course is a course, whether on-line or traditional. . . . Basic evaluation should remain the same. Any other approach would in my view have strong potential to redline on-line courses."

As the discussion progressed, another perspective emerged—what we called the *innovator perspective*—among faculty interested in seeing how this technology could be used to enhance the evaluation of teaching. This position and how it evolved is illustrated as follows:

> "Technology allows us to survey in ways that we have not yet been doing. Here are a few possibilities that I find intriguing:
>
> 1. Survey students about the prerequisite while they are taking the subsequent course.
> 2. Survey students based on various demographic variables that define them rather than by course affiliation, to learn something about the students.
> 3. Survey a cluster of courses to make cross-course comparisons.
> 4. Survey alumni (at least in part as an indirect fundraising tool) [Oct. 21, 1999, male associate professor, economics].
>
> "I agree with all this. One other issue to address in the future: Should TES develop some items that are relevant to on-line courses? This is different than including new items on all on-line forms, and focuses explicitly on on-line courses, or courses that include some students who are on-line" [Oct. 21, 1999, female adjunct instructor, MBA program].
> "This sounds like a good direction on points 1–4. We say 'the on-line course evaluation system.' That could mean either 'the *on-line course* evaluation system' or 'the on-line *course evaluation system*." I assumed more the former, but it's not clear to me why the mechanisms for gathering the evaluation data need to be the same as the methods of course delivery in every case. In fact, I can easily think of exceptions in either direction" [Oct. 21, 1999, male full professor, curriculum and instruction].

We discovered that dialogue and deliberation actually became richer and more complex as issues were discussed. The depth at which issues were addressed increased considerably throughout the four months of discussion. We found, however, that when dialogue and deliberation on an issue were complete, starting new discussion was challenging. Sometimes open-ended questions were a problem on-line, so face-to-face meetings were necessary to reengage dialogue and deliberation. Face-to-face meetings were also critical to present fairly complex material to the group. The on-line group was one of the more successful strategies for creating dialogue and deliberation. During periods of heavy traffic, four or more e-mails per day were sent. Conversely, while the on-line discussion group had the potential to be inclusive, it is not clear that it was; many faculty did not participate ($N = 27$).

The TES faculty review committee has also been quite successful, especially in identifying faculty members' preferences and values. The committee identified a set of issues concerning the evaluation of teaching to review for the campus. For example, working with the evaluation division, the committee recommended to the provost's office that the interpretive framework for department-level indicators of teaching be changed from a norm–referenced to a standards-based approach. The committee also made recommendations about what they valued by what they chose not to change. For instance, in spite of the campus discourse about TES's failure, the committee members felt that adopting additional teaching evaluation methods on a campuswide basis would cut into time that is now spent on teaching and research. The provost's office has approved these changes.

Implementation Issues

> Let us admit that procedures and techniques for meeting these deliberative democratic requirements are more raw, untested, and uncertain than the technical data collection and analysis procedures developed over many decades [House and Howe, 1998, p. 7].

We found implementing inclusion in practice to be challenging. Leveraging participation is complex, creating trade-offs for inclusion. In efforts to ensure inclusion, participation is critical to making sure that stakeholders' perspectives are identified, constructed, and represented. Participation can be either direct (involving all faculty) or representative (involving a smaller number of faculty). We found participation as representation easier to accomplish. For example, administering a questionnaire to all teaching faculty provided everyone an opportunity to have a say (13 percent return rate). Conversely, the focus groups were helpful in providing a broad representation of faculty members' thinking. Participation in focus groups, however, does involve risk and a loss of anonymity for faculty. The questionnaires, which involved direct participation by all faculty, were low risk and anonymous; however, the 13 percent return rate makes the approach a concern. To directly include all teaching faculty in a dialogue about the evaluation of teaching takes either a different method or a more sophisticated approach to questionnaire administration. Possible solutions could be a Web-administered or paper questionnaire sent to all faculty by name, with two or three follow-ups. If this is too expensive or time-consuming, a representative sample of faculty could be administered the questionnaires instead. However, if direct participation is a goal, this will not give all faculty the opportunity to engage in dialogue about the evaluation of teaching.

The focus groups did allow for some dialogue. As a consequence, faculty members' perspectives were clarified (for example, the faculty wanted a standards-based approach). However, to some extent it is more difficult to be inclusive with focus groups. Not all faculty members can participate, nor can all groups. The influence of differential power relationships is also a potential problem in the focus groups. Interestingly enough, more participation (defined here as attendance and involvement in discussion) in the focus groups occurred when the activity was *sanctioned*[7] by authority (for example, when the focus group at a college meeting received a note from the dean indicating his support). However, the quality of the deliberation and dialogue in sanctioned focus groups was distinct from that in focus groups that were not sanctioned by authority (for instance, sanctioned groups did not seem willing to comment about how their teaching was portrayed by the TES).

Whether faculty members perceive a need for additional evaluation approaches has an impact on the faculty members' efforts to participate in the EOn discussion group.[8] In this study, extrinsic rewards (finding a way for on-line teaching to count) may be related to increased participation (Stohl, 1995). Conversely, faculty received only intrinsic rewards for answering the questionnaire that had a low return rate.

The e-mail group, focus groups, and committees have potential for deliberation and dialogue. However, when a focus group is formed around a subgroup (such as the College of Applied Life Studies), no cross-dialogue is possible. It will be interesting to put two stakeholder groups together (such as students and faculty or faculty and administration) to see what kinds of dialogue and deliberation occur.

Nevertheless, we found that the information collected from the diverse groups (such as the EOn discussion group, the TES faculty review committee, the new engineering faculty, and students) and across the different methods (questionnaire, focus groups, and committees) to be rich, complex, and compelling. The creation of these groups and the information collected were critical for building the capacity for faculty members and others to participate in dialogue and deliberation about the evaluation of teaching.

House and Howe's Theory in Practice

> In this conception, the evaluator is not a passive bystander, an innocent facilitator, nor a philosopher king . . . [but] rather a conscientious professional who adheres to a . . . carefully considered set of defensible principles for enhancing inclusion, dialogue, and deliberation" [House and Howe, 1998, p. 6].

The role of the internal evaluator has been the subject of much dialogue and debate within the evaluation community. Because the internal evaluator usually worked for a special evaluation unit within an organization, the he or she was closely aligned with management (Mathison, 1991a). Scriven (1967) proposed that the independence of the internal evaluator was plagued by ambiguity. Further, he suggested that conducting impartial evaluations was logically impossible for internal evaluators. The internal evaluator was summarily dismissed as doing only "formative" evaluation, or the credibility and validity of the evaluator's summative evaluations was questioned (Scriven, 1991).

We do agree that as internal evaluators we find our role to be complex. For instance, in this context, balancing the interests of the client (the provost's office) and stakeholder groups was challenging. However, we find House and Howe's description of the role of the evaluator to be a potential antidote or remedy for some of the criticism historically lodged against the role of the internal evaluator. By redefining the evaluator as committed to the value of advocating democracy and adhering to a set of defensible principles for enhancing inclusion, dialogue, and deliberation, House and Howe (1999) have effectively altered the role of the internal evaluator.

By moving the internal evaluator's role out of alignment with management, House and Howe create a new space for the internal evaluator in which he or she can balance the interests of the client and stakeholders in a more equitable fashion. Nevertheless, there are trade-offs. We found that the boundaries among the client, stakeholder, and evaluator became blurred in this study, for we ourselves became stakeholders in the process in our attempts to democratize the evaluation of teaching.

> How do people participate in the evaluation? The mode of participation is often critical. . . . Getting the correct information requires serious participation from stakeholder groups. . . . How authentic is their participation? How involved is their interaction? [House and Howe, 1998, pp. 6–7].

Where is participation in House and Howe's theory of deliberative democratic evaluation? Participation is woven into the questions that operationalize their deliberative democratic view. Unlike the concepts of dialogue, deliberation, and inclusion, which they specifically define and identify as requirements in their theory, they do not take up participation directly. Is participation, like dialogue, deliberation, and inclusion, a requirement for deliberative democratic evaluation?

We propose that a theory of deliberative democratic evaluation should address participation more directly. Participation is at the heart of deliberative democratic evaluation. We suggest, as House and Howe do in Chapter One, that participation also overlaps and crisscrosses in complex ways with dialogue, deliberation, and inclusion. We find from our study that the participation process is critical. This process can vary in many ways during the implementation of House and Howe's theory; it can take the form of direct participation or participation based on representation; it may be sanctioned or unsanctioned; either extrinsic or intrinsic rewards may be associated with participation; and the extent to which participation in evaluation becomes institutionalized may vary.[9]

House and Howe's theory is a major theoretical contribution leading the way to evaluation in the twenty-first century. As they promise, they provide a guide for the concrete social circumstances in which evaluators practice. What are the next steps? Deliberative democratic evaluation is challenging. When participation is not directly addressed, untangling issues involving inclusion, dialogue, and deliberation is problematic. We propose that a key issue for evaluation theory and practice to address in the new century is the discovery of creative methods of securing representative forms of participation for any group of stakeholders.

Notes

1. Both authors left this evaluation unit in the past year.

2. Kerr (1982) uses this term to describe universities with diverse missions that include commitments to undergraduate education, to research and graduate education, and to the public through service. As a land grant research 1 institution with more than forty thousand students, Midwestern University fits this description.

3. Estimating a precise return rate is difficult given administrative procedures (for example, some faculty may have received two questionnaires).

4. The focus groups included College of Communication faculty ($N = 20$); deans and department heads from the College of Applied Life Studies ($N = 9$); new faculty in the College of Engineering ($N = 20$); the Committee on Excellence in Teaching, College of Agriculture ($N = 16$); College of Applied Life Studies faculty ($N = 40$); the Teaching Advancement Board's campus-level committee ($N = 10$); the TES faculty review committee ($N = 15$); and Latin American Studies faculty ($N = 3$).

5. The members include three administrators (one associate provost and two department heads), four women (one from women's studies), and a faculty member specializing in critical race theory. Members have expertise in qualitative methods, measurement, and statistics.

6. Faculty across campus who participate in on-line or computer-based instruction and all other faculty members were invited to participate in the discussion group. Twenty-seven individuals agreed to participate, including twelve professors, three associate professors, two assistant professors, two teaching assistants, one assistant director, and the authors. There are eight women and nineteen men in the group.

7. Lizanne DeStefano coined the terms *sanctioned* and *nonsanctioned participation* when she reviewed an early draft of this chapter.

8. The School of Library Science and two College of Education departments are interested in investigating technology for evaluating teaching and are quite committed to

seeing EOn that gets off the ground. The fact that they currently have no feasible approach to making their teaching efforts count for their off-campus on-line courses is probably also a factor.

9. During a recent interview with one of the evaluators who remained, we learned that the committees and focus groups with students and faculty are continuing.

References

Braskamp, L., Brandenburg, D., and Ory, J. "Lessons About Clients' Expectations." In J. Nowakowski (ed.), *The Client Perspective on Evaluation*. New Directions for Program Evaluation, no. 36. San Francisco: Jossey-Bass, 1987.

Goodman, P. *The Community of Scholars*. New York: Random House, 1962.

Gray, P. J., and Diamond, R. M. "Defining Faculty Work." In M. K. Kinnick (ed.), *Providing Useful Data for Deans and Department Chairs*. New Directions for Institutional Research, no. 84. San Francisco: Jossey-Bass, 1994.

Greene, J. C. "Evaluation as Advocacy." *Evaluation Practice,* 1997, *18,* 25–36.

Gutmann, A. *Democratic Education*. Princeton, N.J.: Princeton University Press, 1987.

House, E. R., and Howe, K. R. "The Deliberative Democratic View." Presentation at the annual meeting of the American Evaluation Association, Chicago, Nov. 1998.

House, E. R., and Howe, K. R. *Values in Evaluation and Social Research*. Thousand Oaks, Calif.: Sage, 1999.

Kerr, Clark. *The Uses of the University*. Cambridge, MA: Harvard University Press, 1982.

Mathison, S. "Role Conflicts for Internal Evaluators." *Evaluation and Program Planning,* 1991a, *14,* 173–179.

Mathison, S. "What Do We Know About Internal Evaluation? *Evaluation and Program Planning,* 1991b, *14,* 159–165.

Mathison, S. "Evaluation as a Democratizing Force in Schools." *International Journal of Social Education,* 1996, *11,* 40–48.

Schwandt, T. A. "Recapturing Moral Discourse in Evaluation." *Educational Researcher,* 1989, *18,* 11–16.

Scriven, M. "The Methodology of Evaluation." In R. Tyler, R. Gagne, and M. Scriven (eds.), *Perspectives of Curriculum Evaluation*. Skokie, Ill.: Rand-McNally, 1967.

Scriven, M. *Evaluation Thesaurus*. (4th ed.) Thousand Oaks, Calif.: Sage, 1991.

Stake, R. E. "Case Studies." In N. K. Denzin and Y. S. Lincoln (eds.), *Handbook of Qualitative Research*. Thousand Oaks, Calif.: Sage, 1994.

Stake, R. E. *The Art of Case Study*. Thousand Oaks, Calif.: Sage, 1995.

Stohl, C. *Organizational Communication: Connectedness in Action*. Thousand Oaks, Calif.: Sage, 1995.

Strauss, A., and Corbin, J. "Grounded Theory Methodology: An Overview." In N. K. Denzin and Y. S. Lincoln (eds.), *Handbook of Qualitative Research*. Thousand Oaks, Calif.: Sage, 1994.

Wolff, R. P. *The Ideal of the University*. Boston: Beacon Press, 1969.

KATHERINE E. RYAN is associate professor of educational psychology at the University of Illinois at Urbana-Champaign.

TRAV D. JOHNSON is faculty development coordinator at the Faculty Center at Brigham Young University.

5

How can stakeholders be included when deliberative democratic evaluation is carried out in an antidemocratic evaluation?

Surfacing the Realpolitik: Democratic Evaluation in an Antidemocratic Climate

Cheryl MacNeil

I walk through my evaluation site. Having maneuvered the multiple locked doors and security systems at the main entrance, I head toward the unit where my first evaluation participant resides. Down the vast, vacant hallway, I pass large speckled cement pillars and notice the latest construction initiative still in progress; the last outdoor patio is being enclosed with metal bars.

From the wide brick stairwell at the end of the hallway, I look down and see the thick cargo nets that have been strung in the stairwell openings—compensation for an architectural flaw, I presume. Turning at the top of the stairwell, I approach the entryway to the unit where I will conduct my first interview. There is yet another set of double-locked doors. I follow the instructions engraved on the plaque outside the doorway, pressing the buzzer and waiting for a staffperson inside the unit to release the lock. I hear a small electronic hum and pull on the door. I open the door and step into the buffer zone. In front of me is a dense metal door. Thin rows of wire diamonds are latticed within the thick glass of a small rectangular window. I stand in front of the window while the staffperson peers out. As she looks at me, she waits to hear the sound of the first set of doors shutting behind me. At last the interior door to the unit is released. I step through this last door. It closes and locks.

A Response

This is a case study of an evaluation conducted in a psychiatric institution—an antidemocratic climate. The evaluation addresses the three requirements of deliberative democratic evaluation outlined by House and Howe in Chapter

One: dialogue, deliberation, and inclusion. The study illustrates a theoretical justification for stakeholder inclusion from a deliberative democratic point of view (see Chapter Two).

The program I evaluated was a peer-run service for people diagnosed with a mental illness. The program hired people successful in their mental health recovery to work with people who had long histories of hospitalization and were preparing to transition back into their communities. Founded on a philosophy of empowerment, on granting voice and power to those typically disenfranchised, the program seemed to be a coherent match for a democratic evaluation—or so I thought.

As House and Howe have commented, "Evaluation always exists within some authority structure, some particular social system . . . [and] the background conditions . . . under which [such] studies are conducted are critical" (Chapter One, p. 3). Never was there a statement more fitting for my study. Unfortunately, in this setting and others like it, there has been an intermingling of the mental health system with the prison system. Judicial mandates send criminal offenders to seek rehabilitation in psychiatric institutions rather than in existing prisons. This has created a system that mixes the idea of treatment with control and punishment. People seeking help for an emotional or mental illness find themselves sharing space with criminal offenders. As a result, there is a melding of two systems—one that is supposed to punish those who break rules with another that is supposed to provide help. The collective group is subsumed into a larger system that separates all group members from the rest of society and punishes them for breaking laws. The only difference is in which kind of laws are being broken. In the case of the prison system, it is the written laws. In the mental health system, it is the unwritten laws—social deviance from normative customs. Hence, the social consequences are the same for everyone. People become inmates in a highly oppressive system (Jackins, 1991).

There is an important role that deliberative democratic evaluation can play here. It can be responsive in counteracting part of this antidemocratic climate. The evaluation can serve an ameliorative function (Mathison, 1997), assisting to improve the experiences of those who are institutionalized by including them in the evaluation of their program services. Selectively implementing a process of deliberative democratic evaluation can enhance opportunities to promote social justice by granting voice to those of lesser authority (House, 1993).

The deliberative forums I describe in this chapter attended to the presence and participation of disenfranchised individuals in the evaluation of their services, and they demonstrate my explicit value commitment to democratic pluralism (Ryan and others, 1998). By providing opportunities for stakeholders of differing authority to talk with one another in balanced forums, I created inclusive spaces—which previously did not exist. Openly expressing diverse values in a face-to-face interchange among citizens of differing authority, as was the case in the deliberative forums, is an essential ingredient to a democratic society.

One of the major conditions useful for addressing the deliberative democratic agenda in my study was having an established partnership (Mathison, 1994) with the client requesting the evaluation, the program's executive director. Having served as a consultant with the organization over several years, I had a relationship with the executive director and many of the other program stakeholders, and a firm foundation for understanding the organizational context. When the executive director shared with me his disappointment, in both the process and the findings of a survey evaluation he had commissioned in the previous year, I suggested exploring a more participatory approach to designing and conducting the upcoming year's annual program evaluation.

The remainder of this chapter explains my strategies for conducting a democratic evaluation in this highly antidemocratic climate. I spend time describing my processes and methodologies for constructing democratic deliberative forums. I then share participants' reflections about being included in the evaluation.

A Platform for Democracy: Constructing Deliberative Forums

My primary concern in the evaluation of this program was to create inclusive dialogue throughout the process. Driven by my democratic intent, I selected to construct forums that thrived on difference and diversity and that were designed to promote reciprocal deliberation. Constructing forums for dialogue is one approach to addressing the inequalities of power among evaluation participants. As Mathison (1996, p. 2) has claimed, "Deliberation is both a procedure by which we reach a decision and an outcome in and of itself."

Table 5.1 summarizes by dimension the unique characteristics of the deliberative forums in my study. These characteristics were developed in response to some of the shortcomings I was experiencing in conducting evaluations using focus group methodology (Krueger, 1994; Vaughn, Schumm, and Sinagub, 1996). In reformulating attributes of group composition, protocol design features, evaluator roles, and reporting processes, I was able to address better the participatory criteria of a deliberative democratic evaluation. Exploring and analyzing the commonalities of these new reformulations across several evaluation studies resulted in the thematic continuities presented in Table 5.1. These dimensions are what distinguish deliberative forums from other evaluation methodologies. I now explain how these characteristics unfolded throughout my current study.

Table 5.1. Distinctive Characteristics of Deliberative Forums by Dimension

Dimension	Characterization
Methodological Considerations	
Primary intent	Process oriented—enhance democratic deliberative practices; provide voice to stakeholders of differing authority
Point in evaluation process	Emergent—crafted from an unfolding dialogue during the design phase of the evaluation and then reformulated as necessary throughout the process
Investigative process	Perceptions are explored within and across different heterogeneous groups
Issues of Inclusion	
Stakeholder identification	Exponential nomination process via individual stakeholder interviews
Composition of forums	Heterogeneous and diverse groupings; issue dependent, sensitivity to power balance, with weighted representation of disenfranchised stakeholders
Number of participants per forum	Issue dependent, based on vested stakeholder interest
Exploration of the negative case analysis	If identified through initial interviews, is built into the protocol
Deliberative and Dialogic Processes	
Protocol development	Emergent—based on individual interviews with diverse stakeholders; program issues (differences of perception) are identified and provide the framework for the forum protocol
Protocol design	Evaluator crafts key questions to elicit inclusion of those in lesser authority; catalyst for collective and reciprocal deliberation
Evaluator roles and functions	Community builder, conductor, citizen; co-directive and participatory; emphasis on genuine democratic discourse
Reporting format	Designed to meet the information needs of diverse audiences. The same information is distributed to all stakeholders. Multiple feedback sessions include comprehensive findings from deliberations and other evaluative techniques applied throughout the study (such as document reviews, surveys, and observations).
Reporting processes	Promote continual iterative feedback loops with all involved stakeholders; encourage ongoing strategic planning and development

Deliberation and the Realpolitik

Similar to the fourth generation methodology outlined by Guba and Lincoln (1989), I began the evaluation by performing one-on-one interviews with multilevel stakeholders. I especially attended to those who were most disenfranchised, those who were locked up on the units. Starting with individual interviews allowed me to develop an understanding of the different perceptions and issues that would be addressed in the deliberative protocols. To compose balanced forums for dialogue and deliberation, an a priori understanding of where individual stakeholders stood on the issues was essential (see Table 5.1, methodological consideration, point in evaluation process).

The individual interview protocol I developed was a template for soliciting stakeholder nominations and evaluative perceptions about the program. I started the interviews with the obvious stakeholders (program staff, service recipients, and administrators) and used a nomination process from then on, asking each interview participant who else they thought should be involved in the evaluation. In this way I was able to identify an inclusive range of eclectic stakeholders (see Table 5.1, issues of inclusion, stakeholder identification). The process continued until all nominees were interviewed and no new stakeholders were nominated.

I deviated from the fourth generation methodology in my role as an evaluator. In the fourth generation methodology, the evaluator is much like a conduit, gathering, constructing, and conveying information between stakeholders. In my study, I consciously selected not to be the conduit, but rather to be a community builder, bringing different stakeholders together to share with and learn from one and other (see Table 5.1, deliberative and dialogic processes, evaluator roles and functions). This meant crafting deliberative forums based on diversity and composed of stakeholders representing different roles and positions of power and authority within the program. To ensure that the disenfranchised group (those who might typically be excluded or those of lesser authority) would be heard, and to create a power balance, I consciously overweighted the representation of this group in two of the forums. Figure 5.1 illustrates the design and composition of the deliberative forums in relation to the overall evaluation process and the issues surfaced by the individual interviews.

Originally I constructed two planned forums for deliberation of the issues, and later added a third forum after one service recipient's treatment team decided he could not participate in the first forum's deliberation. The forums varied in numbers of participants, depending on the vested interests of the different stakeholders. Invitations to participate in a forum were contingent on the perceptions each stakeholder shared during the individual interviews (see Table 5.1, issues of inclusion, composition of forums). I had identified six thematic areas of perceptual disagreements across the stakeholders that I believed could be addressed in the deliberative forums. In the third forum, I left the agenda open for the excluded evaluation participant to discuss his perceptions.

Figure 5.1. Implementing Deliberative Forums

Promoting Deliberative Democratic Evaluation
Individual Interviews: Stakeholder Nominations, Identification of Claims, Concerns and Issues = Interview Protocol and Topics for Forums Emerge

Forum 1	Forum 2	Forum 3
6 Recipients of Service 2 Administrators 1 Social Worker 3 Program Staff	*5 Current Program Staff* 2 Former Employees 1 Board Member	*1 Recipient* *of Service* 2 Program Staff
Issue A: Paid relationships *Q 1.* Q 2. Issue B: Communication Q 3. *Q 4.* Issues C: Define Success Q 5.	Issue D: Job Design Q 6. Q 7. Issue E: Accommodation Q 8. Issue F: Training Q 9. Q 10.	Issues: Open Agenda Qs.

Report back information to all stakeholders
Ongoing discussion of claims, concerns, and issues discussed with diverse group of stakeholders—generate next steps/future strategies . . .

Note: The italicized stakeholder groups are those identified as disempowered in the context. The italicized questions represent where I specifically designed the protocol to elicit the voice of those most disenfranchised.

Forum 1: "I thought that was very good. That people were given permission to say, 'I don't like how things have been going, I think that there are ways to improve it,' because I think that a lot of people in recovery don't always believe their opinions or experiences are quite as valid as they are and maybe would be a little more reluctant to speak up" [Field notes, administrator, Nov. 17, 1998].

The first deliberative forum addressed three program issues (Figure 5.1, Forum 1, Issues A, B, and C) about which stakeholders held different perceptions: (1) establishing boundaries within paid relationships between the employees and the service recipients, (2) where channels of communication existed and were functional, and (3) the criteria for program success. This last deliberative theme explored the multiple perceptions and definitions related to the program's intended and unintended outcomes (see Table 5.1, deliberative and dialogic processes, protocol development).

I invited six people who received the program services and were currently hospitalized to share their perceptions with a hospital administrator, the service program administrator, a hospital social worker, and three program staff. I consciously chose the same number of people from the disenfranchised group (the service recipients) as from all other stakeholders with authority in the program context.

This is a unique composition given the context. In this psychiatric institution, the service recipient typically sits alone among a sea of professionals, such as in the treatment team meeting. In cases where the number of service recipients tends to outweigh the professional representation, such as in the therapy group, the professional maintains the authoritative status. In the deliberative forums, all were considered equal in voice. As the evaluator and deliberative conductor, I modeled and facilitated this principle by explicating the democratic purpose of the evaluation in each forum introduction, and by being very directive in soliciting the different perspectives throughout the meeting. I was overt and conscious in my intention to create a balanced inclusion of all participant perspectives.

The interview protocol for this forum, and for the others, was specifically designed to engage the disenfranchised group (Figure 5.1, Forum 1, questions 1 and 4) to ensure that their voices were in the mix. As an example, the first question after the general introduction was directed to the people who resided in the institution. The recipients of the program service were asked if they could talk a little bit about how they got involved in the program. In this way, they were cast as credible and vocal participants from the very beginning of the conversations (see Table 5.1, deliberative and dialogic processes, protocol design). The fourth question addressed a different issue but was tailored to serve this purpose as well.

Forum 2: "As the discussion progressed I realized I had a perspective unique to my role that wasn't shared or overlapped by other people even though they were involved and more experienced. . . . It was a different level of perception. Getting all the different players there in the room was very helpful" [field notes, program staff, Dec. 8, 1998).

The issues identified in the second deliberative forum were voiced by employees and related to program policies and practices (Figure 5.1, Forum 2, issues D, E, and F). As such, this forum comprised a mix of program staff. The employees of the program voiced concerns during the individual interviews that part of their job designs were unmanageable, and the program administration needed to explore better ways to accommodate employees who themselves had mental health disabilities. More training was also needed. Although the program administration shared some of these perceptions, they differed in their perception of the balance of supports necessary to meet the employees' needs and the program's needs.

Prior to this group's deliberation, some of the program staff expressed to me concern for their jobs should they voice their opinions too openly. In this regard, I recognized the employees as disenfranchised stakeholders when constructing the forum and the protocol questions (Figure 5.1, Forum 2, questions 6 and 9). One employee spoke to me about not coming at all, and I asked her to think about what it would mean to hear only later about what people said, rather than being there to hear firsthand what people had to say. She thought about that and opted to come, but said she probably would not say anything. Presence is a form of participation, and for some it is enough of a challenge just to be there in such a forum the first time around.

To further equalize the power distribution in this forum, I did a couple of things: I interviewed and invited two former employees to participate in the conversation. This was a very potent strategy to bring the voice of dissension safely into the conversation. These former employees shared the perceptions of some of the current program staff, but they had left the program and expressed feeling less vulnerable about sharing their dissenting perceptions. I also interviewed and invited several of the program's board of directors to participate in the discussion. One of them was able to accept the invitation, and that person's presence had the influence I had planned it to have. My intention in including the board member in the mix was to equalize the administrative power position, to have someone in the forum that the program's executive director was accountable to and under.

These strategies were so effective that they literally reversed the power scales. By the end of the second forum, it was the program's executive director who experienced the tug in the power balance. When I later interviewed him about his participation in the evaluation, he commented, "I wasn't sure what I was getting into and I got more than I expected. I was very pleased with this. It got inside and showed me what I needed to do. It was more probing and uncomfortable than I expected. It is what I want to buy. It is valuable."

Forum 3: "It was good for me to talk to other people. You were able to get them to recognize me" (field notes, Holden, Dec. 8, 1998).

The third forum was specifically designed for Holden, an evaluation participant who was excluded from participating in the first forum. His treatment team had decided he might not be able to manage participating in such a meeting. This was based on their assessment of his ability to be "safe" toward himself or others.

Holden could be considered the *negative case analysis* in the evaluation. Given the analysis of the individual interview data, he was the evaluation participant who held the most opposing and dissenting viewpoint. In other kinds of evaluation he might be considered the *outlier*, "an aberrant case that differs from almost all the other cases" (Weiss, 1998, p. 334), and dismissed for his extreme point of view. Given the criteria of a deliberative democratic evaluation, it was important that inclusion be granted to his lone voice (see Table 5.1, issues of inclusion, negative case analysis).

Unlike the other people receiving program services at the time of the participatory evaluation, Holden was on "constant obs." This meant that at no time was he allowed to leave his double-locked unit without a staff escort. While on the unit, he needed always to be watched by a staffperson. He was under constant observation.

In the context of the evaluation, I framed Holden's position from a democratic inclusive point of view, highlighting his status and the resulting exclusion from participating in the first deliberative component of the evaluation. To compensate for this evaluation exclusion, I arranged for a third, smaller deliberative forum with two program staff and Holden to meet on his unit. In this way he was able to have a face-to-face discussion about his concerns. I invited two program staff hoping that there would be some degree of accountability to each other. I left the agenda open (Figure 5.1, Forum 3) for Holden and staff to discuss a number of his insights and concerns.

Information Dissemination

Reporting back to the participants of the deliberative process was challenging. While trying to meet the information needs of the different audiences, I wanted to make sure that all audiences had access to the same information (see Table 5.1, deliberative and dialogic processes, reporting format and reporting processes). Selectively giving only certain information to one group and not another would serve only to create inequalities in the process. Maintaining a democratic platform during the reporting process meant that I had to communicate all of the evaluation findings to all stakeholders.

I must confess I faltered in my participatory style at this phase and made my reporting decisions in isolation. I decided that I would write a report that was in user-friendly language and could be distributed to all stakeholders. I scheduled open-invitation group feedback sessions, recurring in several different locations (the institution and program offices). All of the evaluation participants eventually had the opportunity to participate in one of the feedback sessions. The discussions addressed the findings of the evaluation, including program areas that evaluation participants agreed were of promise and those of concern, the differences in perceptions on specific issues, and recommendations for future directions. This created further opportunity for reflective deliberation among stakeholders. I considered the reporting process to be yet another forum for creating new beginnings and ongoing dialogue.

Proprietary Liabilities

A month after all of the evaluation participants had received the evaluation report, and after I had completed the verbal feedback loops, I interviewed those who had participated in the deliberative forums about their experiences with the evaluation. The interview protocol contained questions that asked each participant to reflect on their participation in the deliberative forums.

The most powerful impacts reported from participation in this evaluation stem from the dialogic nature of the forums. Participants shared reflections on how their views evolved regarding the importance of their roles, abilities, and responsibilities. As examples, early in the process one program employee commented, "I don't find myself qualified enough to make that kind of judgment. I think that's a question more suited for an executive." Later, after participating in the evaluation, the same employee remarked, "Without the consumer we wouldn't be here, and I work directly for the consumer. I felt important, the hierarchy was inverted for me. I felt more important than the person in the office, even though their role is necessary." Another participant commented, "The hardest part for me was confronting [an individual in the deliberative forum]. I learned about myself that I could voice opinions that I previously may not have had the confidence to voice."

By providing participants at different program levels with an opportunity to hear and discuss the range of perspectives, the evaluation created communal understandings. The same information became available across stakeholders. Participants in the evaluation reported that they had learned how invested everyone was in the program, and how their perspectives were similar to or different from someone else's.

It is unfortunate that in my zeal to conduct the deliberative forums, I inadvertently disenfranchised others from taking on this leadership role. This became apparent when during a postevaluation interview one participant commented, "I'm concerned about whether people in the future can lead these meetings, whether they can establish dialogue." Realizing what had happened, in each subsequent interview I asked participants who they envisioned continuing these sorts of evaluative discussions once I was no longer active in the process. Nobody saw it as their role. I am led to conclude that as a democratic evaluator, I need to be more attentive to opportunities for passing the baton throughout the evaluation process. If I had to do it over, I would have granted more attention to soliciting stakeholder interests in specific evaluative activities, and to coaching individuals at a variety of levels to share the community builder and conductor responsibilities.

Although evaluation participants reported some discomforts and challenges with the process, all remained active throughout the evaluation and reported that the benefits experienced in participation far outweighed the challenges. I had thought that it would be the service recipients who would report feeling most vulnerable during the evaluative process. I was concerned about the potentially intrusive threats that somebody might experience in talking about private circumstances, or the potential threat of sanction if information was disclosed about unacceptable practices (English, 1997). But in the end, participants in this stakeholder group reported that they were able to discuss their programmatic concerns in the carefully constructed deliberative forums.

Those who reported feeling most vulnerable during the evaluation, and whose confidence was most challenged, were the program staff—the program's executive director and employees (Forum 2). I was told that as perspectives became more public by being voiced in the diverse forum, people experienced a greater sense of personal risk and challenge to their credibility. One employee claimed, "I couldn't be just totally candid. I didn't want my comments personalized and [to] jeopardize my future." This participant was distressed by the group composition. He felt intimidated and reserved in the presence of another stakeholder. The deliberative forum suppressed his voice and left him "feeling discouraged and frightened."

This is a lesson in the sustaining power of authority, and in our responsibility as evaluators to continue to support opportunities to practice dialogue among stakeholders of different authority. However, in so doing, evaluators have to be conscious of and accountable for the effects of their evaluative interventions. The appearance of creating balanced or safe spaces for dialogue may be only that, as is the case when a participant is experiencing internal vulnerabilities. In my study, conducting the interviews prior to the deliberative forums was instrumental in framing the different voices into the conversation. Equally valuable were the interviews I conducted after the evaluation regarding participant experiences. These postforum interviews helped to clarify the weight of the constructions presented (or not presented) during the deliberative dialogue, as well as providing participants with an opportunity for debriefing—time to express and alleviate the tensions experienced during the process.

It should come as no surprise that people would feel awkward or not very confident when first introduced to such an opportunity. Recognize how infrequent it is that members of social programs gather in such diverse groupings, especially with this kind of deliberative agenda and equalized composition. It is not common practice. Typically, management or authority figures direct meeting agendas, and their voice has weighted authority. Expressing personal dissension in a public forum, or presenting a point of view different from that of one's superior, is a threatening task for many. The challenges highlighted by the evaluation participants in my study reflect the tensions created when routine group practices are disrupted, when deliberative forums tip the power scales and redistribute voice. Addressing the voice of dissension, or the diminished voice, in this deliberative democratic manner, then, takes practice.

I suggest that in future evaluations exploring the use of deliberative forums it is the evaluator's ethical responsibility to build debriefing opportunities into the design of the study. The evaluator cannot ignore the importance of a trusting relationship with study participants—yet another case for developing sustaining partnerships. As Torres and Preskill (1999) have noted, "The more credibility, trust, rapport, and mutual understanding that exist between and among the participants in an evaluation endeavor, the more successful it seems to be" (p. 64).

References

English, B. "Conducting Ethical Evaluations with Disadvantaged and Minority Groups." *Evaluation Practice,* 1997, *18,* 49–54.

Guba, E. G., and Lincoln, Y. S. *Fourth Generation Evaluation.* Thousand Oaks, Calif.: Sage, 1989.

House, E. R. *Professional Evaluation.* Thousand Oaks, Calif.: Sage, 1993.

Jackins, H. *What's Wrong with the "Mental Health" System and What Can Be Done About It.* Seattle: Rational Island, 1991.

Krueger, R. *Focus Groups.* Thousand Oaks, Calif.: Sage, 1994.

Mathison, S. "Rethinking the Evaluator Role." *Evaluation and Program Planning,* 1994, *17,* 299–304.

Mathison, S. *The Role of Deliberation in Evaluation.* Albany: State University of New York, 1996.

Mathison, S. "Understanding the Ameliorative Assumption in Evaluation." Paper presented at the annual meeting of the American Evaluation Association, San Diego, Calif., 1997.

Ryan, K. E., Greene, J. C., Lincoln, Y. S., Mathison, S., and Mertens, D. M. "Advantages and Challenges of Using Inclusive Evaluation Approaches in Evaluation Practice." *American Journal of Evaluation,* 1998, *19,* 101–122.

Torres, R. T., and Preskill, H. "Ethical Dimensions of Stakeholder Participation and Evaluation Use." In J. L. Fitzpatrick and M. Morris (eds.), *Current and Emerging Ethical Challenges in Evaluation.* New Directions for Evaluation, no. 82. San Francisco: Jossey-Bass, 1999.

Vaughn, S., Schumm, J. S., and Sinagub, J. *Focus Group Interviews in Education and Psychology.* Thousand Oaks, Calif.: Sage, 1996.

Weiss, C. *Evaluation.* Upper Saddle River, N.J.: Prentice Hall, 1998.

CHERYL MACNEIL *is associate director of the Center for Community-Based Evaluations at The Sage Colleges and director of the Recovery and Rehabilitation Training Collective with the New York Association of Psychiatric Rehabilitation Services.*

6

Complexities and confusion surrounding the concept of dialogue are analyzed using a descriptive typology.

Disentangling Dialogue: Issues from Practice

Katherine E. Ryan, Lizanne DeStefano

We see ourselves at the intersection between theory and practice as we write this chapter. Within our own evaluation practices, we are exploring the possibilities and challenges of dialogue in evaluation. We have considered where dialogue fits within practice and how dialogue can be accomplished.

From our perspective, although the notion of dialogue in evaluation is receiving a great deal of attention today, there is a lack of clarity. What dialogue is, whether there is more than one kind of dialogue, and what it can do for evaluation is not clear (Abma, 1998; Greene, 1997; House and Howe, 1998; Mathison, 1996; Preskill and Torres, 1999; Schwandt, 1997). The case studies in this volume illustrate the nature and role of dialogue in evaluation practice.

For example, Greene, in Chapter Two, aspired to a democratic dialogue that encourages a respectful conversation about values and other issues of concern to stakeholders. Although not as successful as desired, she hoped that through these kinds of conversations, groups with diverse perspectives on the issues (science reform and instructional groupings) would learn from each other and come to some common ground. In Chapter Three, Torres, Stone, Butkus, Hook, Casey, and Arens use dialogue for multiple purposes, including the facilitation of organizational learning. Ryan and Johnson, in Chapter Four, were interested in how dialogue among stakeholders might uncover issues of concern that could lead to a broadening of how teaching might be evaluated. And in Chapter Five, MacNeil wanted to create a kind of space for dialogue in which stakeholders of differing status could learn from one another by equalizing power imbalances. She hoped to achieve equality by selecting who participated in the dialogue (more participants from the lower-status group than from the higher-status groups).

New Directions for Evaluation, no. 85, Spring 2000 © Jossey-Bass Publishers

Furthermore, dialogue is currently being considered as an alternative philosophical foundation for the theory and practice of evaluation (Schwandt, 1997). At the same time, dialogue is proposed as a principle means for making decisions that lead to meaningful change, perhaps in society (House and Howe, 1999). For example, Schwandt (1997) has challenged the general logic of evaluation by proposing that evaluation be reconceptualized as dialogic. House and Howe (1999) suggest that dialogue is a critical dimension for conducting democratic deliberative evaluation. While firmly committed to a general logic of evaluation, House and Howe indicate that stakeholder interests, opinions, and ideas can be portrayed more completely through dialogues in the evaluation context. Still others, such as the case study authors (Chapters Two through Five) in this volume, may treat dialogue as a general strategy or even as a technique for addressing issues in the evaluation context (MacNeil, Chapter Five, this volume; Mathison, 1996, Greene, 1997, and Chapter Two, this volume; Ryan and Johnson, Chapter Four, this volume; Torres and others, Chapter Three, this volume).

This chapter seeks to disentangle some of these complexities through a critical examination of dialogue in current evaluation theory and practice. It is organized as follows: First we present some current conceptualizations of dialogue in the evaluation context and at least one from the teaching context (Burbules, 1993; House and Howe, 1998; Karlsson, 1998; Preskill and Torres, 1999; Schwandt, 1997). Next, using a grounded theory approach (Strauss and Corbin, 1998), we develop a provisional descriptive typology for comparing and contrasting current conceptualizations of dialogue. The descriptive typology is based on commonplace notions (such as dialogue goal and process of dialogue) and distinctions identified by Burbules (1993). We then look at the descriptive typology in relationship to two dialogic vignettes from case materials to examine how dialogue is actually accomplished in practice. We close with an agenda for further discussion and future study of dialogue, particularly in the context of practice.

Current Conceptualizations of Dialogue

In this section, we explore how dialogue has been represented in three domains: teaching, evaluation theory, and evaluation practice.

Dialogue in Teaching. Is dialogue a conversation, an inquiry, instruction, a debate, or can it be all of these (Burbules, 1993)? Characterizing dialogue as "a particular kind of pedagogical communicative relation: a conversational interaction directed toward teaching and learning" (p. x), Burbules proposes that dialogue is characterized by two distinctions. On the basis of epistemology, he distinguishes between convergent and divergent perspectives of dialogue. A *convergent* view of dialogue, which presumes that some kind of correct answer can be found or that consensus can be reached, is based on a *teleological* or *referential* view. The *divergent* view is based on Bakhtin's work on language (1986). Divergent dialogue produces multiple interpretations characterized by pluralism, multiple meanings, ambiguity, and complexity.

A further distinction involves an inclusive or critical stance among the participants in the dialogue. A *critical* orientation entails a skeptical and questioning attitude toward what participants are saying to one another. The *inclusive* perspective assumes that what participants are saying is credible, and seeks to understand what leads various participants to their respective positions. These distinctions can be arrayed in a two-dimensional table (Table 6.1) that defines the four genres Burbules identified: dialogue as conversation, inquiry, debate, and instruction.

Dialogue as Conversation. Burbules proposes that divergent, inclusive dialogue as conversation is linked to Gadamer's work on understanding (1982). This genre can be identified by the attitude of tolerance and cooperation and is directed "toward mutual understanding" (p. 112). Critical to this genre is the notion that the understanding is created in the conversation rather than "found." This genre relates mostly to the internal worlds of participants and is useful for clarify beliefs and values. What are the drawbacks of this genre? Although it particularly emphasizes tolerance of other perspectives, there is cause for concern when all positions are accepted with nothing critiqued.

Dialogue as Inquiry. Table 6.1 defines dialogue as inquiry as inclusive and convergent. The aim of this approach is to produce consensus. Although Burbules considers these forms to be highly related, he identifies five forms within this genre: building a common basis for arguments and evidence, solving problems requiring a novel solution, establishing political and social consensus, coordinating action, and addressing moral concerns. The dialogic process is the same for all forms of this genre. By cultivating tolerance and respect for all perspectives, a commitment is made to address an issue of concern and to find some type of solution that is agreeable in part to everyone. Reaching agreement too quickly or making sure that all positions are heard and considered is a potential problem.

Dialogue as Debate. This genre may be used less frequently in the evaluation context as a general strategy. The critical, divergent genre focuses on participants defending their respective positions against the strongest possible challenges. However, although debates can lead to clarification of issues, the intense advocacy positions assumed by participants in a debate tend to lead to I win, you lose kind of thinking, especially in highly-contested evaluation

Table 6.1. Burbules's Four Genres of Dialogue

	Divergent	*Convergent*
Inclusive	Conversation	Inquiry
Critical	Debate	Instruction

contexts. This genre seems most susceptible to contentiousness and argumentativeness, which were identified as issues in an evaluation involving dialogue (see Chapter Two).

Dialogue as Instruction. Table 6.1 identifies the critical, convergent approach as dialogue as instruction. This genre is most closely linked with a Socratic approach to dialogue, in which the teacher leads the student through new and complex learning processes with a set of guiding questions. Although one of the roles of the evaluator is to teach, the evaluator more often helps forge or construct positions rather than lead stakeholders to positions.

Burbules (1993) proposes a number of caveats in considering these genres. He emphasizes that any dialogue will shift into multiple genres and hybrids will occur. In fact, given his developmental characterization of dialogue, he proposes that to move forward in a dialogue often requires that it change from one genre to another.

Dialogue in Evaluation Theory. What we have just described is only a very small part of Burbules's work on dialogue. We find the distinction based on orientation and epistemology particularly useful for our examination of dialogue in evaluation. Here we use these two distinctions to compare and contrast different genres of dialogue in evaluation.

Dialogue as Practical Hermeneutics. Schwandt (1997) proposes moving from a monological notion of evaluation, based on a general logic linked to reason, to a dialogic notion of evaluation. Defining the dialogic notion of evaluation as practical hermeneutics, he suggests that evaluation should focus "on practical judgment and a hermeneutic concern with perceptual knowledge of particularities of concrete situations." (p. 75). Instead of dealing with problem-solving activity, the evaluator is faced with a dilemma that will require understanding and an interpretation that cannot really be derived from an external perspective. This suggests an inclusive stance among the participants in the dialogue. Schwandt proposes that in place of the traditional logic, evaluators should develop practical wisdom. The role of the evaluator is no longer scientific expert; the evaluator is to facilitate conversations, critiques, and alternative perspectives—including a critique of traditional evaluation practices informed by the general logic. The evaluator engages in dialogue with clients and stakeholders about the issues in the evaluation context.

What does this dialogue sound like? This form of conversation is nonauthoritarian. It focuses on education as critical reflection. It acknowledges that there may be no clear answers, which suggests a divergent view of dialogue. In addition, he introduces the notion of *critical intelligence,* which is "the ability to question whether there is a worth getting to . . . the willingness and capacity to debate the value of various ends of practice" (p. 79). This process is essentially a matter of *practical-moral reasoning.* According to Schwandt, critical intelligence based on local hermeneutics can be either a method or a perspective for evaluation.

Dialogue as a Dimension of Deliberative Democratic Evaluation. House and Howe, in Chapter One, propose what they call deliberative democratic evaluation, one component of which is dialogic. They propose that stakeholders must engage in "dialogues of various kinds" to discover their "real interests" through argument or discussion (p. 7). Some of these interests may be constituted in the evaluation itself. Through dialogue, stakeholder interests, opinions, and ideas can be portrayed more completely. The stakeholders' authentic interests and views are represented.

According to House and Howe, evaluators have a special covenant with participants and the public at large because evaluators are "constrained by the value of promoting democracy" (House and Howe, 1999, p. 137). Further, within this conceptualization of the evaluator's role, evaluators should promote an egalitarian sense of justice, be skilled negotiators, and be prepared to take positions on crucial political and moral issues. In efforts to discover or construct real interests, the evaluator is willing to trade some impartiality to gain more understanding of stakeholders' perspectives.

House and Howe's notion of various dialogues is similar to Burbules's notion of multiple genres of dialogue. For example, House and Howe's argument suggests a critical divergent view of dialogue (debate). Conversely, their emphasis on discovering, forging, or identifying "real interests" implies a convergent, inclusive-inquiry approach to dialogue.

Dialogue as Collective Inquiry. In the context of organizational learning, Preskill and Torres (1999) conceptualize dialogue as a collective inquiry in which participants share meanings, ask questions, uncover assumptions, and clarify values and beliefs. A major goal of their notion of inquiry is understanding. They consider dialogue to be different from discussion, which they characterize as an effort to "find agreement, defend one's assumptions, or convince someone of an idea" (p. 54). Their notion of dialogue is most closely linked with what Burbules characterizes as a conversation: a divergent, inclusive dialogue. There is no distinction between internal and external evaluators; the evaluator assumes such diverse roles as collaborator, facilitator, interpreter, mediator, and coach.

Dialogue as a Dialectic Method. To take into account multiple perspectives in an evaluation, Karlsson (1998) proposes a dialogue that is a dialectic method, "critical, conflict-oriented, and not limited to face-to-face relations" (p. 32), which he associates with a Socratic dialogue. The purpose of this particular form of dialogue is for stakeholder groups to share understandings, points of view, and opinions about the positions of respective stakeholder groups, not to reach agreements or consensus, which suggests a divergent view of dialogue.

Karlsson suggests that in order for groups to learn about each other's positions, conflict and critical examination may be a necessary part of the dialogue. However, although different stakeholder groups may not be able to avoid conflict, they would remain on good terms. The goal of critical dialogue is for stakeholder groups to come to more complete understanding of their own positions and the positions of other stakeholder groups. How would this be accomplished? Karlsson characterizes the process as meditative, in which participants critically examine themselves, their own ideologies, and the points of view of other participants.

Karlsson's conceptualization of dialogue is clearly inclusive, but also critical. His description of the dialogue process suggests that the participants may change their orientation during the dialogue, moving back and forth between an inclusive orientation and a critical one, moving from conversation to debate and back again. Karlsson suggests that to facilitate insights and discussion, the evaluator should formulate a framework that situates the program in a historical and political context. He also sees the evaluator as a critical inquirer who emphasizes the complexities involved with making evaluative judgments.

Dialogue in Evaluation Practice. Table 6.2 presents a provisional descriptive typology that compares and contrasts these current conceptualizations of dialogue in evaluation. We acknowledge that these kinds of tables fail to capture theoretical complexity and are oversimplifications of theory. We also recognize that representations like Table 6.2 emphasize differences while failing to surface similarities adequately. House and Howe's, Schwandt's, and Karlsson's views are quite compatible. However, we found this descriptive typology useful for considering the implications of the various conceptualizations of dialogue for practice.

In addition to epistemology and orientation, our analysis includes three common notions, including the goal of the dialogue (what is to be accomplished), the dialogic process (how the dialogue is conducted), and the identity or role of the evaluator, a common concern in practice. For example, as shown in Table 6.2, Schwandt's conceptualization of dialogue is an alternative foundation for considering the conduct of evaluation. House and Howe propose that dialogue is a critical dimension for constituting democratic deliberative evaluation. Through dialogue, stakeholders' real interests are uncovered. Preskill and Torres suggest that dialogue is to be used to uncover assumptions and facilitate reflection (a form of deliberation).

The identity of the evaluator in three of the genres of dialogue is quite diverse, ranging from collaborator, (Preskill and Torres), critical inquirer (Karlsson), and advocate of democracy and negotiator (House and Howe). The dialogue process for both Schwandt's and Karlsson's perspectives emphasize critical examination. However, Karlsson emphasizes a critique of other perspectives while Schwandt focuses on developing alternative perspectives. Conversely, House and Howe propose that the dialogic process is a discussion or argument; Preskill and Torres define their process as "not discussion" and more akin to Burbules's "conversation."

Case Vignettes

We now use this provisional typology to examine two dialogic vignettes from case materials.

Opening the Conversation About the Evaluation of Teaching. This vignette is from the study by Ryan and Johnson presented in Chapter Two

Table 6.2. Descriptive Typology for Comparing Different Forms of Dialogue in Evaluation

	Schwandt	House and Howe	Preskill and Torres	Karlsson
Genre	Practical hermeneutics; model and method	Dialogue as a dimension in deliberative democratic evaluation	Collective inquiry	Dialectic method
Process	A conversation that helps develop alternative perspectives, critical examination	Discussion or argument	Share personal knowledge, ask questions, and seek reasons behind positions	Meditative—stakeholders critique ideologies, themselves, and others
Goal	Dialogue models how knowledge flows from participation	Stakeholders' authentic interests are represented in the evaluation	Understanding	Stakeholders come to more complete understanding of each other's positions
Identity of evaluator	Proposes alternative perspectives, facilitates conversations and critiques	Promote democracy, sense of egalitarian justice, negotiator	Collaborator, interpreter, mediator, coach, facilitator	Critical inquirer
Orientation	Inclusive stance	Critical stance—debate; inclusive forging of interests	Inclusive stance	Inclusive to critical stance
Epistemology	Divergent view	Divergent view—debate; convergent view—forging real interests	Divergent view	Divergent view

that examines inclusion, dialogue, and deliberation in the evaluation of teaching at a large Research I university. The university required all faculty to administer two global items to students as part of its teaching evaluation survey (TES). The evaluators recognized the value of student ratings for the evaluation of teaching and global items. However, Ryan and Johnson wanted faculty to have the opportunity to consider a broader array of choices. An on-line discussion group that would consider how to evaluate teaching seemed a most promising way for faculty to be involved in dialogue about the evaluation of teaching. An excerpt from the dialogue follows, with each e-mail numbered for identification (e-mail 6 omitted because of redundancy):

1. "My preference is therefore that all on-line forms have the two standard items currently preprinted on all TES forms" (Oct. 12, 1999, male full professor, finance).
2. ". . . Also give the instructor the option to make the entire evaluation by herself. On the one hand, it would be good if the instructor took a hands-on view of course assessment as part of a recurrent development process. If possible, that should be encouraged. . ." (Oct. 12, 1999, male associate professor, economics).
3. "Also, some indication of the 'character' of the work might be useful, such as individual or group work, essays or problem sets, textual or graphical data" (Oct. 12, 1999, female assistant professor, library science).
4. "I agree with [the finance professor]" (Oct. 12, 1999, male lecturer, MBA program).
5. "Rather than create another version of an on-line TES, why not get all of us who have developed similar forms together for an hour or two to reach consensus on the form contents" (Oct. 12, 1999, male associate professor, human resources education).
7. "Because these two items are currently used for campuswide purposes—to qualify for the Incomplete List and as longitudinal data in summary reports prepared for P&T evaluations—it is important that our on-line/distance courses also have such indicators" (Oct. 13, 1999, female full professor, library science).
8. "It is possible for the on-line course evaluation system to have alternative items and alternative criteria to qualify for the Incomplete List or other forms of recognition. Alternative items and criteria could also be reflected on the longitudinal profiles for P&T. What are your thoughts on this?" (Oct. 13, 1999, male evaluator, group facilitator).
9. "I agree that TES is a starting point, but of course we will need to add things that address the technology, too" (Oct. 13, 1999, female assistant professor, chemistry).
10. "Technology allows us to survey in ways that we have not yet been doing. Here are a few possibilities that I find intriguing: (1) Survey students about the prerequisite while they are taking the subsequent course. (2) Survey students based on various demographic variables

that define them rather than by course affiliation, to learn something about the students. (3) Survey a cluster of courses to make cross-course comparisons. (4) Survey alumni (at least in part as an indirect fundraising tool) (Oct. 21, 1999, male associate professor, economics).

11. "I agree with all this. One other issue to address in the future: Should TES develop some items that are relevant to on-line courses? This is different than including . . . courses that include some students who are on-line. . ." (Oct. 21, 1999, female adjunct instructor, MBA program).

12. "This sounds like a good direction on points 1–4. We say 'the on-line course evaluation system.' That could mean either 'the [on-line course] evaluation system' or 'the on-line [course evaluation system].' I assumed more the former, but it's not clear to me why the mechanisms for gathering the evaluation data need to be the same as the methods of course delivery in every case. In fact, I can easily think of exceptions in either direction (Oct. 21, 1999, male full professor, curriculum and instruction).

This dialogue tends to resemble the House and Howe approach to dialogue. Although the evaluators used House and Howe's notion of dialogue in considering how to frame the study in general and the dialogue among stakeholders, Ryan and Johnson did not give actual instructions to instructors about how they should talk to each other. The goal of the dialogue was for stakeholders to uncover or forge their real interests through discussion (dialogic process). The evaluators were interested in having the authentic interests of the faculty members represented in the evaluation, and for these stakeholders to find what this might be for themselves. There is a mild tone of debate in some of the exchanges, with two distinct perspectives emerging: traditionalist (student ratings on-line, e-mails 1, 4, and 5) and innovator (innovative evaluation using the technology, e-mails 3, 10, and 12). However, in general there is an inclusive stance—all ideas are considered. We characterize the dialogue as convergent because some form of agreement will be reached on what will constitute the evaluation of teaching on-line. The evaluator was a facilitator, keeping his views out of the discussion and adding commentary primarily for clarification and to move the discussion forward (e-mail 8).

Creating a Context for Dialogue Across Stakeholder Groups. This vignette is from a study by Bresler, De Stefano, Feldman, and Garg (1999) that examines the role of dialogue in an evaluation of the teaching residents (TR) program in a large urban school district. The evaluation of the TR program was commissioned by the TR board to evaluate the program's impact on students and teachers.

Because there were several groups of critical stakeholders, each with a distinct role in the program, members of the evaluation team decided to create the opportunity for dialogue among these groups. The purpose of the dialogue was consistent with that identified by House and Howe, to allow stakeholders to uncover and forge "real" interests that could then be represented in the evaluation.

The four groups that seemed to have primary interest in the TR program and its evaluation were TR staff ($N = 5$), teaching residents ($N = 14$), principals in the schools with residencies ($N = 14$), and classroom teachers working directly with teaching residents ($N = 56$). These groups had never met face to face in the twelve-year history of the program. After much effort, four half-day meetings were scheduled in several strategically selected locations. The dialogue was about to begin.

Authentic Representation. After the first meeting, it became clear that principals and teachers did not view themselves as primary stakeholders in the evaluation. Despite all the prior arrangements, their attendance at the meetings was low. Only one principal and two teachers came to all the meetings. Fewer than half the principals and only a fourth of the teachers came to the meeting. As a result, their perspective was often represented by others:

EVALUATOR: In our interviews with principals, they sometimes reported concern about how much time the Teaching Resident Program is taking away from the general curriculum.

TEACHING RESIDENT: All my principal cares about is whether I have the kids under control.

TR STAFF: Teachers seem to view the residencies more as a free period than a co-teaching opportunity.

Given the lack of principal and teacher involvement in the dialogue, it is questionable whether the goal of authentically representing their interests in the evaluation, at least through dialogue, was met.

In contrast, all TR staff and nearly all teaching residents attended all the dialogue sessions. The evaluators sought to create a context for discussion that was inclusive and convergent. In fact, we hope to use the dialogue to arrive at a set of shared interests around which to structure the evaluation. It soon became clear that stakeholders were quite polarized around the issue of the evaluation itself. The TR staff and a few residents were very interested in doing an evaluation; the majority of the residents were opposed:

TR STAFF: I think the bottom line is, if we can't say that we are making a difference to students and kids, then why are we doing this? Right now we know that we are doing something—but we have no idea if it is making a difference. [1]

TEACHING RESIDENT: So how are going to tell if we are making a difference? What does that mean? If a kid writes a piece of poetry—maybe his first piece of poetry—and he feels good about that, how are you going to measure that? Who is going to say that is enough? Or not enough? You can't measure what we do out there. It is too subtle for the eye. [2]

TR STAFF: That sounds like smoke and mirrors to me. You are in a school for eighteen weeks. At the end, you should be able to point to something you have done. [3]

Through the following dialogue, residents and TR staff were made more aware of (sometimes painfully) each other's perspectives, and the evaluators were sensitized to some program concerns:

RESIDENT: It was almost like group therapy. I said things in there that I wanted to say for years.
EVALUATOR: I felt as if I was watching a family fight. It was intense at times, and personal.

Evaluator's Role or Identity. In addition to playing the observer and data collector role described earlier, the evaluators also found themselves playing a number of supportive and ameliorative roles, such as those described by Preskill and Torres (1999). Originally the evaluators had conceived their role as facilitator (House and Howe) and critical inquirer (Karlsson). Given the contentious nature of the dialogue, the critical role seemed unproductive. As a consequence, when responding to the excerpt numbered 1 through 3, the evaluator assumed the role of mediator.

EVALUATOR: So we have two very different views here [referring to excerpts marked 1 through 3]. [TR staff] seems to be saying that he thinks the evaluation is very important to get his job done. [Teaching resident] seems to be saying that an evaluation is not going to be an accurate portrayal of her work. What can we do about this?

There was no response from the group.

EVALUATOR: Do we all just give up and go home?

There were laughs from group.
A second prevalent role was as coach to participants who were reluctant to speak in dialogue sessions. Because evaluators had the opportunity to talk with participants both individually and in homogeneous groups [residents or TR staff], they were privy to viewpoints that some participants were reluctant to express in the contentious debate sessions:

EVALUATOR: I remember in the focus group, some residents felt that the site selection process was flawed, that TR needed more buy-in from principals and teachers before they place a resident there. Does anyone want to say something about that?
TEACHING RESIDENT: Yeah. When you have the support of the principal and the teachers want you there, it can be great. That's ideal. Without it,

eighteen weeks can be a long time. It's like an uninvited guest who has stayed too long.

Some may criticize the evaluator's active shaping of the discussion as contradictory to the democratic nature of the debate. However, given the threatening climate of some of the dialogue sessions, some issues might never have surfaced without this facilitation.

Although this instance of dialogue in evaluation did not achieve the participation of all stakeholders, or consensus among them, it is illustrative of the ways that dialogue can increase stakeholders' understandings of one another's positions. It also points out the divergent role of dialogue—bringing to light. Finally, as the following resident acknowledged, participants felt included in the evaluation process:

TEACHING RESIDENT: I think it was important to get those things out, with everyone in the room. At least we know what folks are thinking—on the record, you know. It's been said and now it is up to you [the evaluators] to deal with it.

Conclusion

We have worked on trying to understand dialogue in practice. Our provisional descriptive typology framework may be a useful first step in thinking about how to examine dialogue. Framing dialogue in this fashion helped us see that dialogue can and perhaps should take more than one form when addressing even a single issue. Further, in practice we found dialogue most useful for uncovering or forging stakeholders' issues.

We also recognize that there are concerns with dialogue in evaluation, like the problems Greene encountered (see Chapter Two). As a next step in looking at dialogue, we will work with stakeholders to select a specific dialogue approach to use in addressing issues. We expect to outline with stakeholders how this dialogue will be accomplished. This shared understanding about how the dialogue will proceed includes such issues as how conflicts will be addressed, and explicit expectations regarding civility.

Our analysis in this chapter is confined to a microlevel analysis of the dialogic processes in the context of specific dialogic interactions. Schwandt (1997) proposes that the dialogic process is an alternative foundation to the traditional logic of evaluation. We can imagine some kind of parallel macrolevel analysis for examining the structure of the evaluation. House and Howe's examination (1999) of Karlsson's evaluation (1996) is an example of such a macrolevel analysis.

We close with several questions, particularly related to practice. If the major goal of dialogue is discovering "real" interests (as opposed to those that are offered initially), how do we know when we have real issues? What can an evaluator do to make sure that it is possible to address "real" issues within the optimal time frame of an evaluation? What support and training do participants need to engage in the various types of dialogue needed (argument, debate, discussion)? How can we ensure that open dialogue is taking place? What is a good model for this process? Is it like a jury trial with the evaluator as foreman?˙ Or a classroom with the evaluator as teacher?

Abma (1998) has proposed and implemented some imaginative approaches to dialogic report writing. She has also conducted an evaluation of a dialogue to see how participants in a dialogue view the process (Abma, 1999). In this study, the participants expressed concern about a variety of issues: vagueness of dialogue goals, whether the dialogue was open, and who should be a facilitator of dialogue.

We also have concerns about doing nuts and bolts evaluation work. What types of record keeping and information gathering are necessary to facilitate dialogue and incorporate into data analysis and the forging of findings? Who decides what data should be collected? How should information be shared to aid dialogue? What rules should govern access and information sharing (that is, rules of evidence where all parties are given access to all information). Are there general principles here, or is this decided in each evaluation?

In addition to these matters of practice, much theoretical work remains. We propose that a critical concern for evaluation theorists is to explore the meaning of dialogue and the differences in various meanings of dialogue. As Schwandt (1999) suggests, these are conceptual issues relating to the origin and meanings of dialogue and its relevance to evaluation. We expect this work to have important implications for the practice of evaluation.

References

Abma, T. A. "Text in the Evaluative Context: Writing for Dialogue." *Evaluation,* 1998, *4,* 434–454.

Abma T. A. "The Schiphol Discussion: The Future of Dutch Aviation Responsively Evaluated." Presentation at the annual meeting of the American Evaluation Association, Orlando, Fla., Nov. 1999.

Bakhtin, M. M. *Speech Genres and Other Late Essays.* Austin: University of Texas Press, 1986.

Bresler, L., De Stefano, L., Feldman, R., and Garg, S. "Artists-in-Residence in Public Schools." Unpublished manuscript, 1999.

Burbules, N. *Dialogue in Teaching.* New York: Teachers College Press, 1993.

Gadamer, H.-G. *Truth and Method.* New York: Crossroad, 1982.

Greene, J. C. "Participatory Evaluation." In L. Mabry (ed.), *Evaluation and the Post-Modern Dilemma.* Greenwich, Conn.: JAI Press, 1997.

House, E. R., and Howe, K. R. "The Deliberative Democratic View." Presentation at the annual meeting of the American Evaluation Association, Chicago, Nov. 1998.

House, E. R., and Howe, K. R. *Values in Evaluation and Social Research.* Thousand Oaks, Calif.: Sage, 1999.

Karlsson, O. "A Critical Dialogue in Evaluation: How Can the Interaction Between Evaluation and Politics Be Tackled? *Evaluation,* 1996, *2,* 405–416.

Karlsson, O. "Socratic Dialogue in the Swedish Political Context." In T. A. Schwandt (ed.), *Scandinavian Perspectives on the Evaluator's Role in Informing Social Policy.* New Directions for Evaluation, no. 77. San Francisco: Jossey-Bass, 1998.

Mathison, S. "Evaluation as a Democratizing Force in Schools." *International Journal of Social Education,* 1996, *11,* 40–48.

Preskill, H., and Torres, R. *Evaluative Inquiry for Learning in Organizations.* Thousand Oaks, Calif.: Sage, 1999.

Schwandt, T. A. "Evaluation as Practical Hermeneutics." *Evaluation,* 1997, *3,* 69–83.

Schwandt, T. A. "Dialogue in Evaluation: Philosophy, Theory, and Practice." Presentation at the annual meeting of the American Evaluation Association, Orlando, Fla., Nov. 1999.

Strauss, A., and Corbin, J. *Basics of Qualitative Research.* (2nd ed.) Thousand Oaks, Calif.: Sage, 1998.

KATHERINE E. RYAN is associate professor and chair of educational psychology at the University of Illinois at Urbana-Champaign.

LIZANNE DESTEFANO is associate professor of educational psychology, associate dean for research, and director of the Bureau of Educational Research at the College of Education, University of Illinois at Urbana-Champaign.

7

The realities of democracy in the United States have been experientially different for its oppressed groups. How might that affect the practice of democratic evaluation?

Commentary on Deliberative Democratic Evaluation

Stafford Hood

In Chapter One, House and Howe have provided the evaluation community with a thought-provoking framework for judging evaluations in their articulation of deliberative democratic evaluation. Their explication offers instructive advice as to how we might think and behave as evaluators if we are to address evaluation within the American social fabric. It is an ambitious effort to place the mantle of democracy on our evaluative work, because it immediately raises the proverbial bar of expectation.

Deliberative democratic evaluation, as viewed by House and Howe, is synonymous with genuine democracy "because democracy in the fullest sense requires deliberation" (p. 4). Although there may be broad agreement in how democracy is defined and over what it might look like in practice, it is also true that democracy in America has been experientially different for certain groups. I revisit this topic later in the chapter.

House and Howe assert that many evaluators already do much of what they propose in deliberative democratic evaluation through "their own approaches, intuitions, and robust sense of social justice" (p. 3). I concur that certain evaluators appear to employ a democratic approach to evaluation that includes a "robust sense of social justice." I would argue that a robust sense of social justice entails not only a firm belief in the principles of social justice but also meaningful actions that are conducive to achieving

The author would like to thank Terry Denny and Gordon Hoke, professors emeriti, University of Illinois at Urbana-Champaign, for their valuable contributions in the preparation of this commentary.

this end. It has been my experience that evaluations often become political activity that manifests political partisanship or policy advocacy (Wildavsky, 1972), and that such evaluative efforts can be in conflict with the needs and benefits of those who need the most protection under principles of social justice. I openly wonder whether all social justice–minded evaluators have the conviction to address this issue whenever disenfranchised people are concerned.

How evaluative findings might be used is of concern to House and Howe, who maintain that the assumptions evaluators make are important background conditions for evaluation and "should be explicitly democratic so that evaluation is tied to the larger society by democratic principles argued, debated, and accepted by the evaluation community" (p. 4). However, we may want to give further thought to the notion of the evaluation community democratically arriving at conclusions as to how certain evaluation findings might be used. The question arises as to who participates in the democratic evaluation process. The present pool of evaluators of color is woefully small and cannot be expected to be all things to all people or in all places. There simply are not enough such evaluators to go around. So a call for inclusion and fairness, while inherently meritorious, is not enough unless the pool is substantially enriched.

Needed: Program Evaluators of Color

The assumption seems to be that people of color are sufficiently represented in the current decision-making processes. I do not share that assumption. The educational interests of folks of color are not receiving equal protection in evaluation deliberations because they are underrepresented at the table. This is not to suggest that the evaluation community is insensitive to this concern. Having said that, the evaluation community is replete with those who have limited understanding of the values that are grounded in the racial and cultural backgrounds of groups other than their own. Well-intentioned ignorance is my concern here. Martin Luther King Jr. (1963) appeared to have shared similar concerns: "Shallow understanding from people of good will is more frustrating than absolute misunderstanding from people of ill will. Lukewarm acceptance is much more bewildering than outright rejection." Some of my long-standing concerns about the role of cultural bias in measurement (see Hood, 1998a) and evaluation are addressed by House and Howe, who offer deliberative democratic evaluation as an approach to reducing but not eliminating bias in evaluation studies.

House and Howe rightfully acknowledge other evaluators who have similarly sought to reduce bias through their respective evaluative approaches. In my view, the work of Stake (1973), Patton (1994), Fetterman (1994), Kirkhart (1995), and Greene (1997) are notable examples of such efforts. Thus it is reasonable that the three requirements of deliberative democratic evaluation—inclusion, dialogue and deliberation—offer a democratic process with the potential for reducing bias. I take some comfort in the following: "those who have legitimate, relevant interests should be included in decisions that affect those interests . . . [engage in dialogue to discover] what their real interests are . . . [and engage in deliberation that is] grounded in reasons, evidence, and principles of valid argument" (House and Howe, Chapter One, p. 5).

To this I would add additional caveats for consideration, including questions of implementation. I am clear about one fundamental given: my view on democracy is "tinted" by my racial and cultural heritage. I offer this not as an apology for the views I express in this commentary on House and Howe's deliberative democratic evaluation approach. Rather, I provide it as a "readers guide." For some it may be more comfortable to frame my arguments within the construct of critical race theory whereby the law and legal traditions are analyzed "through the historical and contemporary perspectives of racial minorities in this country"(Delgado, 1995). There is a similarity between my arguments and the legal arguments posed by critical race theorists. A convenient label for some, perhaps, but limited for my purpose. Our concerns are grounded in American history: although we had a president who symbolized the freeing of the slaves, we also had one who, during the lifetimes of our grandparents (and some of our parents), joined the Ku Klux Klan. In 1921, President Warren G. Harding allowed himself to be sworn in as a Klansman (Tolson, 1992). In my view, the experience and analysis of African Americans in regard to American democracy is profoundly linked with American slavery.

Race, Democracy, and Program Evaluation

In his speech "What to the Slave Is the Fourth of July?" Frederick Douglass (1852) stated the following:

> What to the American slave is your 4th of July? I answer: a day that reveals to him, more than all other days in the year, the gross injustice and cruelty to which he is the constant victim. To him, your celebration is a sham; your boasted liberty an unholy license; your national greatness, swelling vanity; your sounds of rejoicing are empty and heartless; your denunciation of tyrants, brass fronted impudence, your shouts of liberty and equality, hollow mockery; your prayers and hymns, your sermons and thanksgivings with all your religious parade, and solemnity, are to him, mere bombast, fraud, deception, impiety, and hypocrisy" [para. 46].

These words of Douglass's may be viewed as too harsh for today's America and perhaps for the next millennium. I wish to assure the reader that they are not. I believe it is imprudent to ignore the possibility that for some African Americans, and for others who continue to be disenfranchised in America, Douglass's view may still ring true to their experiences within the

American system of democracy. Given that possibility, does it not follow that democratic evaluative discourse should include those whose life experiences make them familiar with the reality of Douglass's observations?

A more restrained way of expressing Douglass's view may be found in the work of Dubois ([1944] 1985):"democracy is an irrefutable logic, but it calls for intelligence" (p. 237). Intelligent behavior in democratic evaluations requires incorporating the experiences of people of color into the social and institutional structures. Without their inclusion, we fail to meet the basic tenets of deliberative democratic evaluation and of other approaches that hope to reduce bias in evaluative studies.

House and Howe's adamant contention that evaluation cannot be separated from institutional and social structure should not be whispered but rather shouted in the evaluation community. As I have been saying, the issue of race must be placed firmly into this discussion. House's recent work on race and policy lays bare the racist underpinnings of America's social and institutional structures. He observes that he has reluctantly "come to believe racism is deeply embedded within the national identity itself, built into the American character by history and experience" (1999, p. 3). House further notes that African Americans, as well as Native Americans, have played a central role in forming an American national identity by being juxtaposed with an ethnically diverse group of immigrants under the common identity of "white." He acknowledges the apparent permanence of racism in our democracy by citing Jacobson (1998) who asserted, "Racism now appears not anomalous to the working of American democracy but fundamental to it" (p. 12). Although these conclusions are not new, having been expressed by Dubois and others, I commend House for publicly overcoming his reluctance to consider the permanence of racism and its influence on policy. House's previous and most recent contributions to our thinking and work in the evaluation community provide a bridge for us to engage more seriously in a discussion of race and public policy within the context of evaluation.

A first requirement and basic tenet of deliberative democratic evaluation must be inclusion (see Chapter One). The need to include all legitimate and relevant interests while being vigilant in addressing power imbalances is paramount. I do not believe that we should be apologetic in ensuring that the relevant interests of the less powerful stakeholders are protected in evaluative discussions. In this regard I am attracted to Greene's position of *evaluation as advocacy* (1997) and Patton's *developmental evaluation* (1994)—even with the inherent difficulties they have appropriately identified.

A meaningful consideration of the role of race in linking evaluation to American social and institutional structures requires acknowledgment of our need to work toward a critical mass of evaluators of color. Again, Dubois ([1944] 1985) presents a persuasive argument that is useful in the context of deliberative democratic evaluation: "the vaster possibility and real promise of democracy is adding to human capacity and culture from hitherto untapped sources of cultural variety and power. Democracy is tapping the great possibilities of mankind from unused and unsuspected reservoirs of human greatness" (p. 242).

Evaluators of color, largely unused because of their virtual absence from the evaluation community, constitute unsuspected reservoirs for enriching the future of evaluation. Their involvement speaks directly to House and Howe's discussion of the inclusion requirement being instrumental in determining and weighing stakeholders' interests by "distinguishing interests associated with needs from interests associated with wants" (Chapter One, p. 6). Although the matter is complex, we have made a start in examining the evaluator's ability (not desire) to look behind statements of needs to the values that guide them.

Dearden (1968) observed, "But we do not always agree over what is desirable. . . . In such circumstances, it is simply begging the question to talk about needs, or to pretend there is nothing at issue that cannot be settled by empirical research. One has to look behind statements of needs to the values that are guiding them for it is here that the issue substantially lies" (p. 16). The ability to look behind statements of need to the values that guide them, in the case of racial minorities in America, is more likely to occur if the evaluator can draw on shared life experiences as a result of cultural background or extended experiences within a particular culture. Although evaluators of color can make unique contributions in such evaluative efforts, the reality is that we are too few in number. I have written elsewhere about the need for a more concerted effort within the evaluation community toward rectifying this shortage (Hood, 1998b). The need for the meaningful inclusion of evaluators of color should be a facet of the second requirement of deliberative democratic evaluation—dialogue.

The dialogue requirement is an exercise in discovering "real interests" when stakeholders engage in dialogue and deliberation. Dialogue may result in some stakeholders changing their minds as to what are indeed their real interests (see Chapter One). Although it is possible that the evaluator's impartiality might be compromised as a result of extensive dialogue with stakeholders, House and Howe identify what I also agree is a greater danger. They argue, "the greater danger, in our view, is that evaluators will not fully understand the position, views, and interests of the various stakeholders or groups, or that they will misrepresent them in the evaluation. So we are willing to trade some measure of threat to impartiality for the possibility of fully understanding stakeholders' positions by engaging in extensive dialogue with stakeholders" (p. 7).

Dialogue that is predicated on prejudgments of the superior merit of one's view relative to those held by others is doomed to failure. All parties must be open to the possibility that their views are wrong. Only then can they learn from the dialogue. This will be no small task for mainstream, white, male evaluators, or for those traditionally excluded from the evaluative process.

Extensive dialogue with stakeholders does increase the opportunity for a greater understanding by evaluators of stakeholders' true interests. To this I would add that dialogue is an act of communication with both verbal and nonverbal dimensions. In the case of some racial and cultural groups, it is not always what they say but how they say it, as well as the observed nonverbal behaviors. An evaluator of color could play an important role as an "interpreter" in the design stages, during the dialogue process, during the implementation of the evaluation, and in the interpretation of evaluative findings.

The final requirement for deliberative democratic evaluation is deliberation. House and Howe view deliberation as "fundamentally a cognitive process, grounded in reasons, evidence, and principles of valid arguments, an important subset of which are the methodological canons of evaluation" (Chapter One, p. 8). It is indeed a critical element of a democratically minded evaluative approach.

House and Howe's deliberative democratic evaluation approach provides an additional glimmer of hope that the evaluation community can enter the next millennium better prepared to address the challenges that will face us as an increasingly culturally diverse and democratic society. We simply must train and involve more people of color in the process. My continuing call for the inclusion of more trained program evaluators of color does not ignore the goodwill efforts of many evaluators to conduct evaluations that are sensitive to issues of equity and fairness; rather, I find it impossible to discuss American democracy without considering race.

The basic principles of democracy are timeless and precious when we adhere to them in the work we do as evaluators. The constant pursuit of democratic ideals in evaluation and society requires consistent and unwavering commitment or we will lose it. Thurgood Marshall (1978) observed, "It's a democracy, if we can keep it. And in order to keep it, you can't stand still. You must move, and if you don't move, they will run over you" (para. 50). Deliberative democratic evaluation and other evaluative approaches that require the linkage of evaluation to social and institutional structures are examples of action to require the application of democratic principles in evaluation, and consequently result in policy decisions that reflect these ideals. Granting the difficulty of such a pursuit, we can and must continue to invent new evaluative approaches to make our nation's noble democratic ideals a reality for all of its people. As Abraham Lincoln (1860) put it so magnificently, "Let us have faith that right makes might, and in faith let us to the end dare to do our duty as we understand it" (para. 70).

References

Dearden, R. F. *The Philosophy of Primary Education*. London: Routledge & Kegan Paul, 1968.

Delgado, R. "Legal Storytelling: Storytelling for Oppositionists and Others: A Plea for Narrative." In R. Delgado (ed.), *Critical Race Theory: The Cutting Edge*. Philadelphia: Temple University Press, 1995.

Douglass, F. "What to the Slave Is the Fourth of July?" [http://douglass.speech.new.edu/doug_a10.htm]. 1852.

Dubois, W.E.B. Colonialism, Democracy, and Peace After the War." In H. Aptheker (ed.) *Against Racism: Unpublished Essays, Papers, Addresses, 1887–1961, by W.E.B. Dubois.* Amherst: University of Massachusetts Press, 1985. (Originally published 1944.)

Fetterman, D. M. "Empowerment Evaluation." *Evaluation Practice,* 1994, *15,* 1–15.

Greene, J. C. "Evaluation as Advocacy." *Evaluation Practice,* 1997, *18,* 25–35.

Hood, S. "Culturally Responsive Performance-Based Assessment: Conceptual and Psychometric Considerations." *Journal of Negro Education,* 1998a, *67,* 187–196.

Hood, S. "Responsive Evaluation Amistad Style: Perspectives of one African American Evaluator." In R. Sullivan (ed.), *Proceedings of the Stake Symposium on Educational Evaluation.* Urbana-Champaign: University of Illinois at Urbana-Champaign, 1998b.

House, E. R. "Race and Policy." *Education Policy Analysis Archives.* [http://epaa.asu.edu/epaa/v7n16.html]. 1999.

Jacobson, M. F. *Whiteness of a Different Color: European Immigrants and the Alchemy of Race.* Cambridge, Mass.: Harvard University Press, 1998.

King, M. L., Jr. "Letter from Birmingham Jail." [http://www.toptages.com/aama/voices/commentary/bjail.htm]. 1963.

Kirkhart, K. E. "Seeking Multicultural Validity: A Postcard from the Road. *Evaluation Practice,* 1995, *16,* 1–12.

Lincoln, A. "Cooper Institute Address." [http://douglass.speech.nwu.edu/linc_a89.htm]. 1860.

Marshall, T. "Equity Speech: Installation of Wiley Branton, Dean of School of Law, Howard University." [http://www.thurgoodmarshall.com/speeches/equality_speech.html]. 1978.

Patton, M. Q. "Developmental Evaluation." *Evaluation Practice,* 1994, *15,* 311–319.

Stake, R. E. "Program Evaluation, Particularly Responsive Evaluation." Paper presented at a conference on New Trends in Evaluation, Göteborg, Sweden, Oct. 1973.

Tolson, J. *Pilgrim in the Ruins.* New York: Simon & Schuster, 1992.

Wildavsky, A. B. *Evaluation as an Organizational Problem.* London: Centre for Environmental Studies, University of London, 1972.

STAFFORD HOOD is associate professor in the Division of Psychology in Education at Arizona State University.

8

The field has not fully addressed the challenges to the
pragmatic use of democratic evaluation.

Deliberation, Evaluation, and Democracy

Sandra Mathison

> To depend on great thinkers, authorities, and experts is, it seems
> to me, a violation of the spirit of democracy. Democracy rests on
> the idea that, except for technical details for which experts may
> be useful, the important decisions of society are within the capa-
> bility of ordinary citizens. Not only *can* ordinary people make
> decisions about these issues, but they *ought* to, because citizens
> understand their own interests more clearly than any experts.
> —Howard Zinn (1990, p. 6; emphasis in original)

In this volume, House and Howe offer us deliberative democratic evaluation characterized by inclusion, dialogue, and deliberation, an important
but not novel representation of the importance of evaluation in supporting
democracy (see also Greene, 1996; Mathison, 1996a, 2000). This dialogue
is important because it explicitly situates evaluation as a practice that
assumes a political point of view and that is itself value laden (democracy
is itself a value perspective) and that deals explicitly with the values of others. The House and Howe theoretical discussion is complemented by a number of case studies, which in general do not push hard enough or far enough
at the potential that evaluation offers for supporting democratic practices
and creating democratic communities. But therein lies the challenge for
evaluators.

Evaluation has a relatively brief history as a profession and is only
emerging as a discipline. Thus it is relatively easy to see the infusion and
maturation of ideas in the field. One idea that has taken hold is the inclusion of stakeholders. (See Weiss, 1986, for a discussion of the origins of

stakeholder evaluation.) No evaluator would offer up an evaluation that did not at least pay lip service to the notion that stakeholders and their interests ought to be included in an evaluation. There remains, of course, contention about who counts as a stakeholder, just what inclusion means, and the consequences for evaluation when stakeholders are included in novel ways (Mathison, 1996b). For some evaluators, stakeholders are still primarily the people who manage programs and pay the evaluator's bill; but for most evaluators, a much wider net is cast to include program administrators, service providers, and service recipients. And at least a few evaluators work to include (even overrepresent) the typically disenfranchised, the powerless, and the poor. But all evaluators are mindful of the notion of the inclusion of stakeholders.

Stakeholder-inclusive approaches to evaluation attempt to represent the interests and value positions of those with a vested interest in what is being evaluated. Stakeholders are asked by evaluators (through whatever method) what their positions, perceptions, and values are, and evaluators work to represent those views as best they can. Such an approach to evaluation is predictable in pluralistic societies that favor capitalism; interest groups are recognized and prized and the marketplace is where resolutions about competing interests will be made. Many stakeholder-based approaches assume a value-neutral position for the evaluator—the evaluator represents value positions but does not explicitly take one herself. Guba and Lincoln (1989) offer a more dialectical relationship in which the evaluator becomes a sort of conduit among program stakeholders. In collecting the value positions of stakeholders (including her own), the evaluator seeks to confront differences through continuous and repeated dialogue with stakeholders. The evaluator becomes the medium through which stakeholders' value positions are transmitted in an effort to move the understanding of a program forward in beneficial ways.

The Importance of Conflating Dialogue and Deliberation

These perspectives maintain the separation of dialogue and deliberation— dialogue is about soliciting, understanding, and representing stakeholders' value positions, and deliberation is about reasoning about the meaning of these various positions as they inform judgments of the value of a program. The power of deliberative democratic evaluation, though, is in the conflation of dialogue and deliberation, that is, in soliciting stakeholder views in ways that encourage stakeholders to reason about what is good and right, about how they can come to know what is good and right, and about how they might want to make things better. As Zinn suggests in the quote at the beginning of this chapter, responsibility for reasoning about what is good and right is better left in the hands of citizens, with humble support from evaluators.

How might dialogue and deliberation be conflated and how would this increase the democratic potential of evaluation? Here I take democracy to mean something like Dewey's notion of "a mode of associated living, of conjoint communicated experience" (1916, p. 87), or the forms of political action and discourse that Gutmann and Thompson (1996) call deliberative democracy . Democracy is not, therefore, about nation states or electoral politics. It has the potential to exist even in nondemocratic circumstances and states, making the arguments about evaluation and democracy relevant in all contexts.

First, what is meant by deliberation? Deliberation, it seems to me, presupposes what Fay (1987, p. 179) calls an "activist conception of human beings," that is, people are (at least potentially) broadly intelligent, curious, reflective, and willful beings. These natural tendencies, Fay contends, are awakened in noncoercive contexts and constitute a rational response. "To be rational is to have good reasons for one's beliefs, together with an openness to reconsider alternatives and a willingness to revise one's beliefs if evidence is adduced which fits better with an alternative system of beliefs" (p. 179). Deliberation, then, assumes a capacity for empathy and requires a willingness to engage in a dialogue with others about beliefs, with the real possibility of revising those beliefs should the evidence warrant it.

Deliberation is only one of several means by which we can reason about something to arrive at a conclusion, almost invariably an evaluative claim. For clarity, deliberation can be contrasted with two other common forms of reasoning—negotiation and demonstration. Negotiation is a strategy familiar in labor-management bargaining that intends to reach a compromise acceptable to both sides. There are accepted rules for negotiating and in general the parties approach each other as adversaries, each side expecting to make compromises that will result in an acceptable if not perfect outcome. Demonstration relies on authority and tradition to reach a conclusion. For example, it may be shown that through time an enduring understanding has become the case and therefore we decide to agree based on existing institutional practices that something is and ought to be the case. Deliberation, by contrast, is regulated by three principles—reciprocity, publicity, and accountability. "Reciprocity asks us to appeal to reasons that are shared or could come to be shared by our fellow citizens" and to assume that knowledge claims are "consistent with reliable methods of inquiry, as these methods are available to us here and now, not for all times and all places" (Gutmann and Thompson, 1996, pp. 14–15). Deliberation takes place in public forums, or at least is disseminated in public forums, and accountability is achieved through challenges to positions, evidence, and justifications in these public forums.

If the conditions of inclusion, dialogue, and deliberation lead to democratic practices and arrangements, then who better to do the dialoguing and deliberating than stakeholders—with one another, supported by but not filtered through the evaluator, the distant expert who is well meaning but always in danger of misunderstanding the interests of citizens. It is not necessary or desirable for evaluators to speak for others, especially those who are disenfranchised (the mentally ill, the elderly, children, teen mothers) or different from the evaluator (people of color, the working class, the less formally educated). It is necessary for evaluators to work in ways that permit and facilitate opportunities for these stakeholders to dialogue and deliberate with one another about all the elements of the evaluation process we understand to be critical as expert evaluators.

It seems that the editors of this volume want to make a distinction between what is here called deliberative democratic evaluation, and empowerment-oriented participatory evaluation. Such caution seems unnecessary. An empowerment-oriented participatory evaluation may or may not be democratic. For example, an empowerment evaluation focusing on the emancipation of a particular disenfranchised stakeholder group (be it women, children, the homeless, or Hispanics) may purposefully eschew democratic practices in order to give voice to this stakeholder group. However, any deliberative democratic evaluation must by definition be empowering. If such an evaluation does not disrupt the balance of power with an eye to redistributing that power, then democracy will not be served.

For fear that the discussion in this volume provides great promise with little hope for pragmatic use of deliberative democratic evaluation, I will end on an optimistic note. Although the challenges to deliberation and to democracy in general are great and real, the power of citizens to represent their interests, to participate in deciding how to live a life worth living, remains evident. I am heartened by my involvement with a growing grassroots movement of parents and teachers throughout the country who are engaged in resistance to high-stakes standardized testing in schools. Much of the work of this movement is accomplished through dialogue and deliberation, with a substantial infusion of expert advice. Evaluation as a profession can and should work within these contexts, as well as those funded, aided, and abetted by governments, corporations, and foundations, and in so doing has even greater potential for contributing to the principles of democracy.

References

Dewey, J. *Democracy and Education.* New York: Free Press, 1916.

Fay, B. *Critical Social Science.* Ithaca, N.Y.: Cornell University Press, 1987.

Greene, J. C. "Qualitative Evaluation and Scientific Citizenship." *Evaluation,* 1996, 2, 277–289.

Guba, E. G., and Lincoln, Y. S. *Fourth Generation Evaluation.* Thousand Oaks, Calif.: Sage, 1989.

Gutmann, A., and Thompson, D. *Democracy and Disagreement.* Cambridge, Mass.: Harvard University Press, 1996.

Mathison, S. "Evaluation as a Democratizing Force in School." *International Journal of Social Education,* 1996a, 11, 40–48.

Mathison, S. "The Role of Deliberation in Evaluation." Paper presented at the annual meeting of the American Evaluation Association, Atlanta, Nov. 1996b.

Mathison, S. "Promoting Democracy Through Evaluation." In D. Hursh and E. W. Ross (eds.), *Democratic Social Education*. Bristol, Pa.: Falmer Press, 2000.

Weiss, C. "The Stakeholder Approach to Evaluation: Origins and Promise." In E. R. House (ed.), *New Directions in Educational Evaluation*. Bristol, Pa.: Falmer Press, 1986.

Zinn, H. *Declarations of Independence: Cross-Examining American Ideology*. New York: HarperCollins, 1990.

SANDRA MATHISON is associate professor of educational theory and practice at the State University of New York at Albany.

9

Five themes illustrate different dimensions of the process of diffusing democratic deliberation into widespread use.

Benefits and Limitations of Deliberation

Gary T. Henry

In Chapter One, House and Howe provide an engaging and intellectually intriguing model for rescuing values from their current confused state in evaluation. By confronting the dismissive "just the facts" position of logical empiricists and the radical relativism of both constructivists and postmodernists (House and Howe, 1999), deliberative democracy offers a justification for selecting some criteria for judging program performance over other criteria. The justification is procedural in that it specifies process criteria, and it is supported by a firm theoretical base in that it descends from well-regarded theories of deliberative democracy (Bohman and Rehg, 1997; Benhabib, 1996; Habermas, 1996).

Indeed, it is difficult to quibble with linking evaluation to democratic processes. Evaluation, as House and Howe note, is an influential institution within modern democratic societies (Chapter One; see also Henry and Julnes, 1998; Mark, Henry, and Julnes, 2000). The argument advanced by House and Howe is that by strengthening the internal procedures of evaluation to make them more democratic, evaluation can better serve democratic institutions. That is, by becoming more deliberative, evaluation can provide less biased information to the institutions that are charged with choosing among various policies or programs of action and to those that who carry them out. Because a main theme of this volume is the diffusion of democratic deliberation into more widespread use, I have organized my comments around five alliterative themes that are tied to realizing this potential: appreciation, addition, apprehension, application, and adaptation.

Appreciation

First, I wish to recognize and properly appreciate the contribution made by House and Howe. In Chapter One, these authors have raised reason to an honored position in the conduct of evaluation. Prior to their attempt to bring procedural requirements into play as important elements for justifying the selection of some criteria over others in an evaluation, the values component of evaluation suffered from extreme biases of two sorts. From one perspective, there was no way to justify the use of one groups' values over those of another group, so the choice was arbitrary and it was left to the evaluators to decide which group should be privileged. From the other perspective, values were mostly taken to be self-evident and were chosen without much reflection. House and Howe (Chapter One; also, 1999) offer a third alternative. Inclusive dialogues that are deliberative can provide justification for the value positions employed in evaluation. In a parallel manner, procedural requirements have been available and used by evaluators for the collection and analysis of information and are used to justify the superiority of some information over other information. House and Howe have begun the movement toward raising values to the same level as facts in the practice of evaluation.

This movement has important implications, including regarding values as findings. By conceiving of values identification as findings, House and Howe bring into focus concern for the rigor that is required to support the selection process. Heretofore there was near-universal agreement that stakeholder involvement was an essential component of an evaluation, but the selection and involvement was highly variable and often idiosyncratic. At this early stage in the development of deliberative procedures, there may be disagreements about whether an evaluation was inclusive or not and about exactly what it means to be inclusive, but evaluators have a point of departure for our debates about whether an evaluation was rigorously conducted with respect to values. This should add immeasurably to our ability to make progress on this front.

Additions

Deliberative democracy, as it is currently described, will need to confront some apparent limitations, such as the number of circumstances in which it can actually be applied in its current form, and perhaps the number of situations in which it is actually necessary. I take up these two issues under the general topic of additions that are necessary to consider as the theory is developed.

For evaluations of local programs—where a community exists prior to the evaluation and where a solid representation of community members, including those who have been directly affected by the program, can be organized—the evaluation should be able to proceed with deliberative procedures. A prerequisite for deliberation, according to Cohen ([1973] 1997), is that the group engaged in deliberation is committed to advancing the common good. Without a sense of interdependence and real commitment to resolving differences through deliberation, the possibility is slight that reason rather than individual interests will carry the day. In other contexts, this sense of shared interests is referred to as social capital. Social capital consists of rational actions whereby investments are made in other members of the social network who experience obligations and expectations of reciprocity (Coleman, 1988; McNeal, 1999). Putnam, Leonardi, and Nanetti (1993) have found that social capital explains the effectiveness of other democratic institutions (such as regional governments in Italy), and it is likely to be necessary for the success of deliberative evaluation.

For programs of metropolitan, state, or national scope, it is difficult to imagine the ties of social capital being strong enough to cause the common good to emerge as an overriding concern during the course of a single evaluation. In the largest effort at deliberation to date, Fishkin (1995) organized a "deliberative poll" to allow a representative group of Americans to deliberate on issues prior to the 1996 presidential election. The representatives were selected in a manner that maximized inclusion and they engaged in a substantial amount of public dialogue, from small group sessions to expert panels to exchanges with presidential and vice presidential candidates. However, few opinions shifted as a result of the deliberations (Merkle, 1996). The strength of identity politics and opinions that have formed through natural processes that preceded the deliberations may be very hard to change without substantial prior investment in social capital.

We can describe the deliberative processes called for by House and Howe as methods of stimulating or simulating the process of opinion formation about public issues. These processes do not enter a vacuum. Opinions exist prior to deliberation, and much social research indicates that resistance to change is an important motivation in accessing, attending to, and processing information. These difficulties cannot be ignored and are likely to be pronounced during the relatively short run of most evaluations. The lack of social capital as well as the lack of long-term consequences for maintaining prior opinions could lead to dissention more than consensus. Greene, in Chapter Two, provides an illustration of this outcome in which individual interests are not checked a substantial investment in social capital or a high degree of commitment to the process. Conversely, Johnson and Ryan, in Chapter Three, seemed to be working in an environment where a commitment to the process was in place, social capital existed, and the deliberative processes worked more smoothly.

The second addition that seems to require some elaboration of the model focuses on the issue of whether deliberation is needed in all evaluations. Elsewhere my colleagues and I have argued that where natural valuation processes have already crystallized, it may not be necessary to deliberate (Henry and Julnes, 1998; Mark, Henry, and Julnes, 2000). It may be sufficient to tap the existing value positions across diverse groups (Henry, 1999). In addition, others have pointed out the need for evaluation to assess the outcomes in particular contexts and the moderating effects of different contexts (Pawson and Tilley, 1997). Choosing valued outcomes that have been used in prior evaluations may be very important to advance our knowledge of the effects of programs. This type of evaluation would not necessarily require deliberative procedures to establish the criteria for success, but deliberative democratic procedures could be a useful addition in these evaluations, especially at the conclusion and recommendation stages of the evaluation process. In other words, democratic deliberative criteria may add rigor to some evaluations, but they need not be a part of all evaluations.

Apprehension

I have one central apprehension about deliberative procedures: the lack of attention given to collecting information that is as unbiased as possible to inform the deliberations. One can read the deliberations to include three steps: identifying high-priority criteria for judging program success, measuring performance for each of the high-priority criteria, and reaching judgments about the program based on the performance information across all of the high-priority criteria. Though it is unlikely that the steps will be taken in a linear fashion, they still need to be accomplished. In some cases, it seems possible, although from my point of view unlikely, that the entire evaluation can be self-contained in this way. It is more likely that a division of labor, which Habermas (1996) also anticipates, will be necessary that separates the gathering of information on performance from the deliberations concerning values and the how public action should be programmed. In an example that appears in House and Howe (1999, p. 126), information external to the current evaluation, presumably unbiased information from another evaluation, is interjected into the deliberations by the evaluators. Information is critical to the deliberation process and it cannot be assumed to arise solely from the deliberations themselves. Democratic evaluation should not give short shrift to producing information that measures program performance that is as unbiased as possible and that will assist others with their roles in making democracies work.

Application

As the chapter authors note, the examples of deliberative democratic evaluation presented in this volume used procedures that were generally consistent with the tenets and criteria, but they were not necessarily developed with the three procedural guideposts. For example, Torres and her coauthors (Chapter Three) did not try to achieve the inclusiveness standard advanced by House and Howe in Chapter One; therefore it is not productive to judge how well the evaluation met this standard. In future applications, success at achieving a representative group for deliberation using one strategy or another will need to be compared and contrasted as well as assessed for adequacy. The same is true for neutralizing preexisting power relationships in dialogues and ensuring that those with minority opinions engage with others rather than recede from the debates or appear to agree, which was a specific concern for MacNeil (Chapter Five), for which she advanced a specific strategy. It cannot be assumed that all attempts to implement deliberative evaluations will be close-enough approximations of the ideal to justify the findings that emerge. Honest appraisals of the success of various strategies and approaches will be needed to speed application and improve the rigor of the findings generated through democratic deliberations.

Adaptations

Deliberative procedures will have to be adapted to be used in some evaluations. For example, state or federal evaluations often are too geographically dispersed to allow for face-to-face deliberations. Dialogue at the national level, as Fishkin (1995) has shown us, is at least daunting and at worst downright impossible. Furthermore, we must begin to countenance the likelihood that explicit trade-offs will need to be made in adapting the procedures to real evaluation situations. For instance, is it better to achieve a more inclusive representation of participants or to have greater depth of dialogue? Other researchers have argued that deliberations will of necessity be mediated (Page, 1996). One way to assess this is to ask how sound the justification is for choosing criteria for judging program success when one or more of the procedural requirements for deliberative democratic evaluation are relaxed.

Conclusion

House and Howe have rendered invaluable service to the field of evaluation by indicating the importance and indeed the possibility that evaluators can justify their choice of criteria to judge the success of programs, and by specifying procedural criteria that will support the justification. Their work should be viewed as a starting point for further development of the procedures that can justify the selection of performance criteria. Much work remains to determine how to apply and adapt the criteria to diverse evaluation contexts and purposes in addition to the assessment of merit and worth.

References

Benhabib, S. (ed.). *Democracy and Difference: Contesting the Boundaries of the Political.* Princeton, N.J.: Princeton University Press, 1996.
Bohman, J., and Rehg, W. (eds.). *Deliberative Democracy: Essays on Reason and Politics.* Cambridge, Mass.: MIT Press, 1997.

Cohen, J. "Deliberation and Democratic Legitimacy." In J. Bohman and W. Rehg (eds.), *Deliberative Democracy: Essays on Reason and Politics.* Cambridge, Mass.: MIT Press, 1997. (Essay originally published 1973.)

Coleman, J. S. "Social Capital in the Creation of Human Capital." *American Journal of Sociology,* 1988, *94* (Suppl.), S95–S120.,

Fishkin, J. S. *The Voice of the People: Public Opinion and Democracy.* New Haven, Conn.: Yale University Press, 1995.

Habermas, J. "Three Normative Models of Democracy." In S. Benhabib (ed.), *Democracy and Difference: Contesting the Boundaries of the Political.* Princeton, N.J.: Princeton University Press, 1996.

Henry, G. T. "What Do We Expect from Preschool? A Systematic Inquiry into Values Conflicts and Consensus." Paper presented at the annual meeting of the American Evaluation Association, Orlando, Fla., Nov. 1999.

Henry, G. T., and Julnes, G. "Values and Realist Evaluation." In G. T. Henry, G. Julnes, and M. M. Mark (eds.), *Realist Evaluation: An Emerging Theory in Support of Practice.* New Directions for Evaluation, no. 78. San Francisco: Jossey Bass, 1998.

House, E. R., and Howe, K. R. *Values in Evaluation and Social Research.* Thousand Oaks, Calif.: Sage, 1999.

Mark, M. M., Henry, G. T., and Julnes, G. *Evaluation: A Realist Approach—Description, Classification, Causal Analysis, and Values Inquiry.* San Francisco: Jossey-Bass, 2000.

Merkle, D. M. "Review: The National Issues Convention Deliberative Poll." *Public Opinion Quarterly,* 1996, *60,* 588–619.

McNeal, R. B., Jr. "Parental Involvement as Social Capital: Differential Effectiveness on Science Achievement, Truancy, and Dropping Out." *Social Forces,* 1999, *78,* 117–144.

Page, B. I. *Who Deliberates? Mass Media in Modern Democracy.* Chicago: University of Chicago Press, 1996.

Pawson, R., and Tilley, N. *Realistic Evaluation.* Thousand Oaks, Calif.: Sage, 1997.

Putnam, R. D., Leonardi, R., and Nanetti, R. Y. "Making Democracy Work: Civic Traditions in Modern Italy." Princeton, N.J.: Princeton University Press, 1993.

GARY T. HENRY *directs the Applied Research Center in the Andrew Young School of Policy Studies at Georgia State University, where he also serves as professor in the Department of Political Science, Department of Public Administration and Policy Studies, and Department of Educational Policy Studies.*

10

To what limit may professional evaluators promote deliberative democracy?

A Modest Commitment to the Promotion of Democracy

Robert E. Stake

The purpose of program evaluation is to acknowledge merit and shortcoming, not to promote democracy. To claim, as Ernest House[1] and Kenneth Howe have in the first chapter (and similarly elsewhere; see House and Howe, 1999, forthcoming) that "evaluation in democratic societies should aim for. . . fostering deliberative democracy" (Chapter One, p. 4) is to risk misrepresenting the work of professional evaluators. Also, House and Howe's zealous rallying is troublesome, and their claim that democracy needs to be deliberative needs to be challenged.

Of course, there are more than single purposes in complex inquiries. Beyond judging the quality of various aspects of the program, evaluators are expected to provide information for understanding, accountability, and decision making. They are expected to support the ethical, professional, and cultural values of those with whom they work. Evaluators are expected to teach others how to improve evaluative operations within their programs. In practice, there is no single purpose of evaluation. House (1974, 1979, 1980) has been one of the best at describing the complexities of the work of the evaluator. Certainly the promotion of democracy can sometimes be an ancillary purpose.[2]

Evaluation designs and operations have political, economic, and social implication, and it is not improper for evaluators to hope that their evaluative work will contribute to the amelioration of social distress. It is also not improper to go a bit off the main track toward that end, or for individual evaluators to promote any political philosophy, as long as that intention is widely made known.

New Directions for Evaluation, no. 85, Spring 2000   © Jossey-Bass Publishers

Not a Matter of Choice

House and Howe indicate that evaluation cannot help but encounter democracy, at least indirectly, and that what evaluators have done during the study and how they arrange dissemination of findings implicates democratic philosophy and practice. To play no role in furthering or foregoing democracy is not an option. The formal evaluation of a public program obligates the evaluators to consider their contribution to social and political life.

House and Howe call for evaluators to declare their commitments. We should not expect to succeed at this. Our expertise in this business tells us that routine declaration of values tends to be selective and self-serving. Still, it should be apparent from our portfolios how dedicated to public issues we are. Some individual evaluators will announce and aspire to the promotion of democracy. Others will not, some for good reason.

It would contribute to oversimplification and misunderstanding were we to set as a major and general aim of program evaluation the promotion of democracy. As with many social service professionals, evaluators have the privilege of directing a portion of their work toward aims other than those commonly expected, especially when the aims are consistent with the aims of stakeholders. So a modest effort by an evaluator to contribute to deliberative democracy or another ideology can be defended, but a vigorous political advocacy by the community of professional evaluators would stand a good chance of violating public expectation and confidence.

Social Expectation

It is essential for evaluators to be attentive to the language of stakeholders, clients, and the public. When it is said that a program has been evaluated, there is warranted expectation that the operations, management, accomplishment, cost, and ethics have been scrutinized. It is less common but not uncommon to expect that steps toward program improvement have been identified, that future decisions have been facilitated, or that management has been helped to be more rational. It may be part of the contract or merely part of the work ethic. The term *evaluation* has common meaning; its denotations and connotations should seldom be neglected when providing evaluative services to distant audiences.

In education and social action programs, the constituencies, purviews, aims, and standards are sufficiently varied and ambiguous so that no two evaluators are expected to use the same design and the same data resources, and to make exactly the same interpretations. Evaluations are expected to reflect the disciplinary origins and cultural experiences of the evaluators. Some would say there ought to be greater standardization, but at the present time standardization would probably be achieved at the cost of sensitivity and service to diverse communities. There is room for evaluators to be different, but not so different that what has been promised to be evaluative turns out to be something else.

When an official announces that a program has been evaluated and found to be to some degree effective, it is a mark against the profession if public expectations of coverage have been disregarded, no matter how meritorious the other contributions.

MacDonald's Democratic Evaluation

Twenty-five years ago, when Barry MacDonald (1973, 1977, 1978a, 1978b) introduced the concept of democratic evaluation, he defined it largely in contrast to bureaucratic evaluation and autocratic evaluation. He saw the pursuits of ordinary people, of government agencies, and of academic researchers (funded by the government) as sufficiently different to require different designs and different handling of evaluative inquiries. MacDonald did not claim that bureaucracies were indifferent to the needs of ordinary people, but he noted that consistently the use of evaluation studies by agencies was to further the immediate interests of the agency. "[The evaluator's] techniques must be credible to the policymakers and not lay them open to public criticism" (1977, p. 226). The fact that the agency's long-range mission was to serve its constituents, often a sector of the public, did not, MacDonald found, obligate it to direct its evaluation commissions to be of most use, or of any use, to the public. Frustrated by government ownership of studies and selective disclosure of findings, MacDonald (1999) now indicates that it is important that some evaluators commit themselves to providing information that is useful to the public.

It has long been apparent to MacDonald that the business of evaluation is often associated with academic studies and that many evaluation studies exist more for the furthering of science, public policy, and other ideational systems than to serving the information needs of the public. Academics, even when (as in Britain recently) denied traditional support and respect, can use their disciplines and media for expressing concerns and for the pursuit of their values. Although it is not uncommon for the welfare of the people to be identified in their exchanges, this academic design of research, and of autocratic evaluation in particular, as practiced so far, does not sufficiently consider the importance of a well-informed citizenry. In 1973, MacDonald concluded that a different kind of program evaluation was often needed to provide to the public good information about public programs.

MacDonald did not base democratic evaluation on needs assessment or participative evaluation. He felt that seldom should part of a study's budget be spent assessing needs, because knowledge of needs was available through existing research, ordinary political processes, and literary channels.[3] He did not expect that it would serve an inquiry well to share responsibilities for design and operation with stakeholders. He allowed that it might be of value to individual stakeholders to participate, but that the well-being of the various stakeholder groups could be better served by the evaluator's well-deliberated choices of issues, data sources, and reflective conversations.[4] It is easy to read House and Howe as calling for participative evaluation.

MacDonald treated democratic evaluation as a self-discipline for the evaluator. House and Howe (Chapter One) have endorsed that same self-discipline but they go further, calling for a professional movement, urging individual evaluators to make explicit their links to the larger sociopolitical structure. They urge the collectivity of evaluators to argue, debate, and accept a commitment to fostering democratic principals. MacDonald would say that the general welfare can be served by public involvement in evaluative studies, but that he cannot do his best evaluative work by making management of the evaluation a participative process.

MacDonald has not always been satisfied with the American way of saying things, so upon reading the draft of this chapter, he sent me the following clarifications (personal communication, Nov. 25, 1999):

1. The purpose of programme evaluation is to promote knowledge of the programme on the part of those who have a right to know, or the duty to advise, or the obligation to provide, or the power to stipulate. Prioritisation of audiences depends on context and opportunity variables.

2. Democratic evaluation is most appropriate in contexts where there is widespread concern about new developments in the management and control of education (e.g., Thatcher's New Right). It is also appropriate in circumstances where institutions are seeking to establish new organisational forms that are less hierarchical, more collective. In these circumstances, highly participative approaches may be appropriate.

3. Promoting knowledge should stop short of advocating courses of action. Our job is to inform debate, not to preclude it. Modesty is called for.

4. We see power in action. In most if not all programmes we see injustices in how power is exercised. In all the cases I can think of, the misuse of power is detrimental to the realisation of the programmes' stated aims. In drawing attention to malpractices of various kinds it is difficult to separate democratic values from concerns for programme effectiveness.

5. Most of the evaluations I do offer some opportunities to invite significant participants to think again about how they discharge their responsibilities. Evaluation should be educative in intent, and this should be evident in its processes. Micro impact is as important as macro, maybe more so.

6. I do not seek confrontation with the powers that be, but challenge is sometimes unavoidable. Mine is a hundred year project, not a quick fix.

Democracy

The democratic ethic calls for serving the well-being of the collective and of each individual. The practice of democracy is arranging for the expression of preferences by each individual and honoring the majority. In this real world, it is easy to see that the majority is often inconsiderate of the remainder. Democratic practice does not necessarily reflect democratic philosophy. Following John Rawls, House (1976) defined democracy philosophically, urging maximum good across maximum numbers. It is a political ideal to which most evaluators are sympathetic, although at least on occasion they carry on evaluation studies indifferent to the well-being of the broadest group of stakeholders. This in spite of the American Evaluation Association's "guiding principle" that states (Shadish, Newman, Scheirer, and Wye, 1995, p. 20): "Evaluators should articulate and take into account the diversity of interests and values that may be related to the general and public welfare."

Like House and Howe and MacDonald, Jennifer Greene (1997) advocated that evaluators make explicit value commitments, expecting that most would find it hard to justify any other than democratic values. Recognizing that consciously and unconsciously, intentionally and unintentionally, we evaluators regularly respect personal and own-group value positions, she said we ought to increasingly attend to value positions of those who are suffering societal inequities and injustices. Again, like House and Howe and MacDonald,[5] Greene said that evaluators should try to redress some of the power differential in political affairs. She noted (personal communication, Nov. 29, 1999), "A program is judged to be 'good' when it fairly and equitably addresses all legitimate stakeholder interests, when it advances democratic aims of justice, when it involves interactional and relational processes of respect, caring, reciprocal learning and understanding." Others urging an ethic of caring within evaluation include Gilligan (1982), Noddings (1984), and Newman and Brown (1996).

Greene used the term *pluralistic democracy* rather than deliberative democracy, concentrating on the people to be served rather than on the essentiality of deliberation. Ensuring appropriate issues and providing information are very different aims than fostering deliberation among the people. Is it really the business of evaluation to promote program rationality and public discussion, however desirable they might be?

Like all the evaluation theorists, Saville Kushner (forthcoming) acknowledged the inevitability of the intrusion of evaluator values into the evaluative act. Indeed, he argued that methodology should be thought of as a means of reconciling the twin demands of the evaluator's own values in respect for social justice and the characteristics of the field under study. He too stopped short of proposing that evaluation move into advocacy, even short of evaluators burdening the stakeholder with their own views. For Kushner, the values of the evaluator help to define the shape and conduct of the inquiry, but they should not intrude on its substantive business. The evaluator's values as to social justice may determine, for example, that the interview is an essential instrument for exposing the plurality of individual voices in a program—even in balancing weaker voices against stronger. But evaluators have no warrant, he has said, to import those values into the process of making judgments. As long as findings are generated and published in a

democratic crucible of discourse, and as long as a plurality of views is represented, Kushner would argue that even the most unpalatable program outcomes and positions should be promoted through evaluation.

The great problem for many evaluators is that democratic respect for
the values of the man and woman in the street requires tolerance, sometimes
acceptance, of simplistic views. When one has studied the complex
processes of education or social service at length, the majority opinion is
often dismaying. In theory, the democratic view can be held dear and an
effort can be made to teach something better, but in the final chapter of the
evaluation report it is difficult to pay full respect to a popular view that is,
to the evaluator, absurd. For example, in America today the popular view
(as well as the government and the corporate view) of educational accountability is that standardized achievement test scores indicate the quality of
teaching at a school. To go well beyond mere acknowledgment of this view,
to embrace it so as to contribute to democratic processes, is not an acceptable choice for many evaluators.

MacDonald (1978a) spoke of the democratic evaluator as a broker,
exchanging information between groups who want knowledge of each
other. John Elliott (1977) chided MacDonald for feeling obligated as a
democratic evaluator, as earlier, to promote interests that differ from the
evaluator's own. Elliott correctly pointed out that democracy requires tolerance but not advocacy of others' interests. An evaluator should be driven
by professional responsibility to focus on merit and shortcoming. It is hard
to see how an evaluator following House and Howe's advocacy could serve
the interests of the citizenry without casting those interests in a favorable
light.

Activism

House and Howe are bold in their advocacy of democratic philosophy. But
they have refrained from the boldness of many in the activist community.
They avoid identifying measures for evaluators to help directly those who
lack justice. The two of them would have us be industrious and ingenious
in including evaluative questions that are attentive to the plight of the
afflicted, but they do not endorse favoring the afflicted in data analysis or
interpretation. They do not advocate obscuring data that are unfavorable
to the cause. They do not urge us to advocate the case of the poor, wanting
merely to have that case emerge if a more or less value-free data analysis
will allow it to do so. They do not suggest that the injustice is ever so great
as to warrant action ordinarily considered unethical. Theirs is not a shrill
call for revolution. They seek less than activism for democracy; they seek
activism for turning the profession toward greater sensitivity to the needs
of democracy.

If this is activism, it is a literary one. House and Howe call for critical
redirection, the endorsement of qualitative deliberation. It is a movement

away from impersonal indicators of merit toward merit as seen in personal experience. They endorse inclusion, dialogue, and deliberation.[6] These are indeed important mechanisms for both evaluation and democracy. Recognition of multiple realities, multiple cultures, and a broad range of stakeholders is synonymous with House and Howe's appeal for inclusion. Triangulation, narrative, and negotiation are other words for dialogue, and deliberation is a common expectation of formal evaluation, justifiably admired by House and Howe both in the personal domain of reflection and in the institutional domain of meta-evaluation. In evaluation, as in political process, these are commendable ideals, a suitably modest commitment to democracy.

There is also the matter of evaluator behavior in an environment of misuse of information, including misrepresentation of evaluation findings. In an e-mail message (Dec. 2, 1999) drawing my attention to a key aspect of MacDonald's thinking, Kushner called it

> the hardest piece of the democratic pemmican to chew on. The democratic evaluator having "no concept of evaluation misuse" and the evaluator eschewing a public deliberation role are not likely to be central players in follow-up to the report. This may become significant in extreme circumstances. For example, the systematic corruption of research evidence by the British government to promote deeply ideological views of curriculum and assessment in the guise of value-free, technical indicators leaves the democratic information broker looking somewhat hapless. In such a situation, might post-study deliberation, democratic interactivity, and activism become an *obligation* on evaluators?

To me, the question is, should advocacy of democracy and activism for justice be part of my professional behavior or done by me outside it? It will happen both ways, but I can vigorously mix them or try to keep them separate. House and Howe and others advocating democratic evaluation argue for the vigorous mix. I oppose it. I am sure that evaluators, as professionals, should at times violate pledges and contracts when a greater moral principle is at stake—for example, violating a confidentiality promise in order to report serious immoral administrator behavior. But to advocate ideology or to battle political corruption, I think it is best to step out of the professional role. I believe that professionals can best make their twin contributions by trying to keep the two roles separate.

Deliberation

As with activists generally, House and Howe zealously urge each evaluator to move to their ideals. But do we believe that if a little change would be good, universal change would be better? It will serve evaluation well to be more modest, to recognize the great power in deliberative schemes, but to recognize the costs as well. Legislative process, the courts, the sciences, and the media all showcase deliberative processes—ones that blind as well as illuminate, suspend action as well as enrich it, and oversimplify as well as draw out new complexities. Some evaluators should promote a deliberation ethic; others should oppose it.

But indeed, dialogue, deliberation, and dialectic processes are underplayed in ordinary evaluation work (Proppé, 1979; Stake, 1998). Meta-evaluation should be not only an independent gathering of key data (Scriven, 1969) and checking against standards for the conduct of evaluation (Stufflebeam, 1975), but also reflection and critical review of interpretations, enhanced by dialogue with those who hold other points of view. Deliberation is needed not only to nurture democratic values but also to understand the merit and shortcoming of the evaluand.

Good evaluation practice goes hand in hand with contribution to the promotion of deliberative democracy within programs and across societies. But it is better that evaluators play no greater than the modest role advocated by MacDonald in furthering democracy. While going about the business of evaluating programs, they should attend first to their contracts, to public expectation, and to their professional obligations.

Notes

1. With Barry MacDonald, House was discussing these issues in the mid-seventies, writing of them in his treatment of John Rawls's position on justice (House, 1976). With Kenneth Howe he has moved beyond his earlier views.

2. The multiplicity of purposes increases as evaluation is a corporate or institutional activity. In their writing, House and Howe speak of evaluators as professionals or entrepreneurs more than as workers highly dependent on the company. According to Mac-Donald and Norris (1978), increasing corporate domination of evaluation limits bargaining power.

3. The concept of needs is a difficult one. Acknowledging complexity, uncertainty, and controversy, House and Howe say that "evaluators must design evaluations so that relevant interests are represented" (Chapter One, p. 6). They follow Bhaskar (1986) and Scriven and Roth (1976) in seeking to identify interests that attach to needs, which they contrast with wants and preferences, which are what the needy speak of. Needs are regularly what somebody else thinks the needy lack. But which of us does not see something we badly want as a need? And if evaluators are not ready to let the needy define their own needs, where is the democratic ethic? The resolution for evaluators is to hear the pleas, to deliberate, sometimes to negotiate, but regularly, nondemocratically, to decide what the relevant interests are.

4. David Jenkins, Stephen Kemmis, and Roderick Atkin (1977), working with MacDonald on the UNCAL project, found three dilemmas: (1) between the stakeholder's right to know and the project's right to be discreet, (2) between independence and responsiveness, and (3) in being democratic while trying to provide a test of the democratic model.

5. In his original writing, MacDonald (1978a) argued for evaluation based on the concepts of confidentiality of data, negotiation, and accessibility of findings to stakeholders, with the key ethic being one of "the citizenry's right to know."

6. Following Amy Gutmann (1987), House and Howe claim in Chapter One that democracy requires joint deliberation by citizens on matters of social policy. It is likely

that this is a definition less favored by those who are not much into deliberating. In a deliberative democracy, do the taciturn get half a vote?

References

Bhaskar, R. *Scientific Realism and Human Emancipation*. London: Verso, 1986.

Elliott, J. "Democratic Evaluation as Social Criticism, or Putting the Judgment Back into Evaluation." In N. Norris (ed.), *Safari Theory in Practice*. Norwich, England: Centre for Applied Research in Education, 1977.

Gilligan, C., *In a Different Voice*. Cambridge, Mass.: Harvard University Press, 1982.

Greene, J. C. "Evaluation as Advocacy." *Evaluation Practice*, 1997, *18*, 25–35.

Gutmann, A. *Democratic Education*. Princeton, N.J.: Princeton University Press, 1987.

House, E. R. *The Politics of Educational Innovation*. Berkeley, Calif.: McCutchan, 1975.

House, E. R. "Justice in Evaluation." In G. V. Glass (ed.), *Evaluation Studies Review Annual*, vol. 1. Thousand Oaks: Sage, 1976.

House, E. R. "Democratizing Evaluation." Paper presented at the annual meeting of the American Educational Research Association, San Francisco, Apr. 1979.

House, E. R. *Evaluation with Validity*. Thousand Oaks, Calif.: Sage, 1980.

House, E. R., and Howe, K. R. *Values in Education and Social Research*. Thousand Oaks, Calif.: Sage, 1999.

House, E. R., and Howe, K. R. "Advocacy in Evaluation." *American Journal of Evaluation*, forthcoming.

Jenkins, D., Kemmis, S., and Atkin, R. "An Insider's Critique." In N. Norris (ed.), *Safari Theory in Practice*. Norwich, England: Centre for Applied Research in Education, 1977.

Kushner, S. *Personalising Evaluation*. London: Sage, forthcoming.

MacDonald, B. "Briefing Decision Makers." In E. R. House (ed.), *School Evaluation: The Politics and Process*. Berkeley, Calif.: McCutchan, 1973.

MacDonald, B. "A Political Classification of Evaluation Studies." In D. Hamilton, D. Jenkins, C. King, B. MacDonald, and M. Parlett, *Beyond the Numbers Game*. London: Macmillan, 1977.

MacDonald, B. "Evaluation and the Control of Education." In D. Tawney (ed.), *Curriculum Evaluation Today: Trends and Implications*. London: Macmillan, 1978a.

MacDonald, B. "Democracy and Evaluation." Public address at the University of Alberta, Edmonton, Oct. 17, 1978b.

MacDonald, B. Statement on the occasion of his investiture as Doctor Honoris Causa, University of Valladolid, Spain, Nov. 9, 1999.

MacDonald, B., and Norris, N. "Twin Political Horizons in Evaluation Fieldwork." Paper delivered at a conference, The Study of Schooling: Field-Based Methodologies in Educational Research, organized by the Wisconsin Research and Development Center for Individualized Schooling and held at the Wingspread Conference Facility, Racine, Nov. 1978.

Newman, C., and Brown, R. *Applied Ethics for Program Evaluation*. Thousand Oaks, Calif.: Sage, 1996.

Noddings, N. *Caring: A Feminine Approach to Ethics and Moral Education*. Berkeley: University of California Press, 1984.

Proppé, O. "Dialectical Evaluation." Urbana: University of Illinois Center for Instructional Research and Curriculum Evaluation, 1979 (mimeo).

Scriven, M. "An Introduction to Meta-Evaluation." *Educational Product Report*. 1969, 2 (5).

Scriven, M., and Roth, J. "Needs Assessment." *Evaluation News*, 1976, *2*, 1–4.

Shadish, W., Newman, D., Scheirer, M., and Wye, C. (eds.). *Guiding Principles for Evaluators*. New Directions for Program Evaluation, no. 66, San Francisco: Jossey-Bass, 1995.

Stake, R. "Some Comments on Assessment in U.S. Education." *Educational Evaluation and Policy Analysis,* 1998, 6, 14.

Stufflebeam, D. *Metaevaluation.* Occasional Paper Series, no. 3. Kalamazoo, Mich.: Evaluation Center, 1975.

ROBERT E. STAKE is professor of educational psychology at the University of Illinois and director of CIRCE.

INDEX

Back Issue/Subscription Order Form

Copy or detach and send to:

Jossey-Bass Inc., Publishers, 350 Sansome Street, San Francisco CA 94104-1342

Call or fax toll free!

Phone 888-378-2537 6AM-5PM PST; Fax 800-605-2665

Back issues: Please send me the following issues at $23 each
(Important: please include series initials and issue number, such as EV77)

1. EV _____

_____

_____

$ _____ Total for single issues

$ _____ Shipping charges (for single issues *only;* subscriptions are exempt from shipping charges): Up to $30, add $5^{50} • $30^{01}–$50, add $6^{50} $50^{01}–$75, add $7^{50} • $75^{01}–$100, add $9 • $100^{01}–$150, add $10 Over $150, call for shipping charge

Subscriptions   Please ❏ start ❏ renew my subscription to *New Directions for Evaluation* for the year ____ at the following rate:

❏ Individual $65   ❏ Institutional $118

NOTE: Subscriptions are quarterly, and are for the calendar year only. Subscriptions begin with the spring issue of the year indicated above. For shipping outside the U.S., please add $25.

$ _____ Total single issues and subscriptions (CA, IN, NJ, NY and DC residents, add sales tax for single issues. NY and DC residents must include shipping charges when calculating sales tax. NY and Canadian residents only, add sales tax for subscriptions)

❏ Payment enclosed (U.S. check or money order only)

❏ VISA, MC, AmEx, Discover Card #_____ Exp. date_____

Signature _____ Day phone _____

❏ Bill me (U.S. institutional orders only. Purchase order required)

Purchase order #_____

Name _____

Address _____

_____

_____

Phone_____ E-mail _____

For more information about Jossey-Bass Publishers, visit our Web site at:
www.josseybass.com   **PRIORITY CODE = ND1**